CHANCE OF RAIN

Catherine D'Angelo Meade

ISBN: **1542548977**
ISBN 13: **9781542548977**

In Loving Memory of
Mary Pauline Weinrich Meyer

Grandma, in answer to your repeated question,

"Yes, I *am* writing a book."

TABLE OF CONTENTS

PROLOGUE

After Andy died, I allowed myself only ten days to think and cry and pray and wonder. I am a teacher. Teachers plan. I expected to be finished cleaning up the mess that memorial services leave in just ten days. That was the plan: back to school for all of us in ten days.

For those first days without Andy, I did not answer the phones that rang and rang. I did not want company that didn't mind tears on their shirt. I didn't want to talk with anyone who did not understand what it felt like to truly love Andy and then lose that. I just didn't want to be with anyone.

On those days, God was kind. The weather was perfect, especially for mid-April. I was able to wear shorts in the stillness of the backyard patio and even begin to tan. I sorted through some mail, wrote out some thank you envelopes, but overall, I did nothing. I sat in the nothing while the birds built their houses and chirped along to the sound of spring and life. I smelled the air that Andy couldn't. It was hard, but necessary work, this grieving. I had to allow myself to do nothing for this little bit of time.

As I sat, you'd think I would have cried out, "Why?" to God. I didn't, though. In fact, I was a little surprised by this myself. I thought that I would want answers. I thought that one of the stages of my grieving would include this need to be angry with God and demand answers. That's just not how it happened for me.

I had a different question for God. I asked Him what I should do. I wanted to know how to go on. The bills. Oh, the bills! There were so many: medical bills, credit card bills, utilities that were ready to be turned off, insurance payments, car payments, and the mortgage! Oh, the mortgage! It was looming over me. We were almost in foreclosure with no hope of recovery. Without Andy's salary, we had a household income reduced by half. There was a lot to consider and a lot that caused concern. (Choosing *concern* is my way of skirting the word *worry*, because I try to tell myself that excessive worry is a sin. It *is*. It's me not trusting God as I should. It's kind of a running theme for me.) Anyway, I was *concerned*. I asked God what to do. I asked the air what to do. I asked myself what I should do. I asked the absent Andy what I should do. Then, I only sat and waited and listened. Eventually, quietly, I felt that I got my answer. The answer was writing. I felt it. I knew it. I was to write. I had to write. That was the whole answer. Nothing more.

There was a financial decision to make, though. How will I pay the bills, and how will I earn money? I have young kids here at home who are grieving. I am grieving. Andy's daughter, Katie, is also grieving. I wanted details. "How is this going to pay the bills, God? If I write every day like I feel led to do, if I stay home from summer school like I feel led to do, then I will actually make my financial position worse, won't I?"

Still, I continued to get the same feeling. As I sat and thought and prayed and grieved and cried, the same thought kept running through my head. I know God speaks to me this way. I can miss it sometimes; I mistake it for my own voice or for the voice of doubt and fear that can creep in, but this was God. I felt much peace over this ridiculous decision to skip out on summer school and write. That unexplainable peace that comes is God-given. I didn't know what I was to write, but I had an answer. I had a wonderful sure feeling that I needed to write. Humph. Write?

"So, what should I write, God?"

No answer.

That's all God gave me. I was sure that I would write for the summer of 2008. So, here it is, July 27th. I am writing.

I told my family that I would skip my paying job at summer school and write instead. Being a new widow, there's not a lot that people will disagree with me about. No one wants to be the one to upset me. They are afraid of setting me off. I have seen this when I just feel like crying and the last person who speaks to me feels responsible. They apologize like crazy and really look like they feel guilty about it. They carry it on into the next time I meet them sometimes, too. It's such a strange phenomenon – this being a new widow thing.

I'm sure that people are happy to see me moving toward something productive and positive, and they may think that encouragement is the way to go. Some people have seemed truly excited, too. To me, I know it is the right choice. To soften the blow, I explain to myself that I will treat this like work. "I will get up daily at 5:30 am. I will write until the kids get up. That's three hours of writing at least for each day – that's just like putting in hours at summer school." I tell myself and others that I will treat this like a commitment to an outside job.   I reason that I can sell whatever I write. Maybe.

From a financial point of view, deciding not to teach this summer is a terrible idea. How can I even consider staying home and writing instead of going out for a pay-check? Childcare issues aside, it's a no-brainer. I should get to work to try to prevent foreclosure. The family is depending on me only now. Except that now I just have this strong feeling that writing is the answer. It's about trust.

Heavenly Father, please hear my prayer. I want You to direct my thoughts and ideas each step of the way with this book. I am so blessed to be given this task. Please teach me, Lord. Help me, Lord, to get myself out of the way. Show me how to give myself over to Your direction. I pray for clarity and for peace and for perseverance. I pray that You will grant me the ability to discern what is meant to be said and what is not. Please bless this family as I begin. Help, Lord. Send mercy to us all. Send me Your grace and goodness each morn-ing.   Lord, help me to keep my eyes on You only these days and to remain focused on the message You are giving me. Help me to remain in Your Spirit as I write. Keep me from distractions. Grant me patience and more love to put toward the running of this home. Keep Your Spirit nearby as I walk through the days of summer. Bless our time together, Lord. In Jesus' name, Amen.

I have to go to sleep now. I'm so excited to be writing that I'd like to stay up all night. My eyes won't have it though. They want to sleep. As Andy would say, "I have lead." That means, my eyelids are as heavy as lead.

I have lead. More tomorrow.

1

THE WAKE

I awoke that morning with a song in my head. I wasn't sure if I had been dreaming the song, but I knew that my spiritual DJ was playing it for a purpose. Whatever the reason, it was stuck in my head. It kept playing on and on. The song was familiar, but I didn't know the lyrics. All I knew was the tune. I hummed it out loud as I reached for Andy's ipod on my nightstand. As I looked through, I found the song I heard. The Beatles. Of course. "I'll Follow the Sun." I scrolled through and found other songs that were meaningful to us. Katie, our 19-year-old, made a playlist and prepared the portable ipod dock to play those songs throughout the wake. Perfect. Andy would exit this world with music in the room.

Next, I chose clothes for all three kids; I chose clothes for myself. I ironed everyone's dark colors, found socks, shoes, stockings. *"Keep busy. Don't dwell on it."* I also chose clothes for my husband to wear for the viewing. I laughed with Katie about it because I'd chosen to bury her Dad in his 'clown pants' as she and I called them: his beloved, too-big boxers with the huge navy blue polka dots. He liked to wear them around the house. He also thought they looked enough like shorts to pass for outerwear. Katie and I did not agree with him. We openly taunted him about it often. He was even caught several times on the front lawn in them. Naturally, for the wake, he wore them *under* his suit. No one knew about them but me, Katie and the undertaker.

I did my hair. I put on make-up minus the eyeliner and mascara that crying wouldn't stand. I chose open-toed shoes even though April on Long Island isn't really warm enough for that. Andy had always admired my polished toenails. From the house, my daughters and I went straight to the nail shop in town and had our toes done. My extended family thought it odd that I had planned to spend most of the morning primping myself and the kids in a manner that suggested relaxation. Relaxation was not my purpose, though. It was different. It was the last time I could dress up for my husband. It was the last time the kids could dress up for him, too. We were expected to impress his family and friends with our poise and appearance and strength. That would have made him proud of us. I felt that. The toenails polished and ready made me very confident that he was smiling and approving of us. Silly. I know that. It was part of the process for us, though.

I distracted myself and the kids on the way into the funeral home. We carried armfuls of things intended to decorate the room. We even brought origami paper cranes that Andy's students had folded – one thousand of them! – in wicker baskets. His students had read *One Thousand Paper Cranes*, a story where a girl folded cranes in the hopes that she would be granted the wish of a full healing from cancer, a Japanese folk custom. Like Andy's story, that book ends with a funeral, too. We also brought photo boards and albums and framed pictures. We brought the stereo for the ipod to play the music. Our arms were full. My brain was busy planning how to decorate, and I guess I'd hoped to keep the kids busy with this part of it, too. That did not work out at all. Even now, I still don't know where those items were put, how they were displayed, or even if they were ever arranged at all. I walked into the viewing room and promptly fell apart – all thoughts of poise and calm and remaining available for my kids left me. I was suddenly completely crippled by the real-ity of my husband in the casket.

The viewing room felt tremendous to me then. I really had that tunnel vision I'd only heard of before now. The room distorted: much, much longer than it had been. In my memory I can only see a long narrow room with Andy's casket at the far end of it. The flood of tears and that awful sound that came with it are a strong and awful memory. "What is Andy doing up there? He looks like he's just sleeping! If I try to wake him up and I find that he's dead, I know it will be too much to bear. Help me, Lord." And help, He did. The Lord sent our family and our friends in the right order and in the right timing to hold me and hug me and comfort me.

First, my brother cried with me. He helped me up from where I was crouching child-like on the floor and sat me down in a chair. Then Katie fell apart, too. She needed me to gather strength to give to her. I did. Next I started to make my way to the casket with the help of Andy's best friend Tony. He kept his arm around me and guided me and whispered comfort to me that I cannot even remember now. Andy guided him for me. I stood at Andy's casket quietly weeping expecting to have a chance to collect myself there before people began to arrive. I was wrong.

In what seemed like only a moment's time – before I'd even started to understand that Andy wasn't going to get up, someone told me it was time to turn around and face the room. It was time to take my place as the grieving widow and allow the mourners to greet me and offer condolences. This shocked me for some reason. I wasn't ready. I could not accept that I was really going to greet people. I was really going to share this awful mess with everyone. It was very suddenly real.

I turned to see Maggie looking at me, the first in line. She is a teacher from my building, a co-worker, a friend, a caring woman who had come in kindness to console me with her sincere apologies for my sorrow. I knew she was kind. I knew she was sincere. I knew she was coming out to console me. I just could not accept that this was so bad that people who knew me only through work would be there. "This is really bad," I kept thinking. "If people I've never seen outside of work are here, this is really bad." It was then that I lost my balance a bit. I don't know if I would have fallen like so many stories of the dramatic Italian widow, but I am grateful that Tony still held my waist. He ushered me to sit in that big, fat armchair designated for me. I cried and cried in the arms of my co-worker who bore much more of the brunt of my grief than she was ever meant to. I will never forget her, surely another angel sent by the Lord.

Katie set up the music. We greeted people. Many, many people came. Co-workers of mine, co-workers of Andy's, a busload full of current students, prior students, family, friends, neighbors, even doctors came. I laughed with most. I comforted *them*. I encouraged them to cry because of how healing it is. I told them that this was sad and that we were *supposed to* cry at times like these. I told them that Andy had a merciful end. I told them how beautiful it was and how much it had reminded me of a birth. I told them we were sad, but we were okay. I told them this was the most beautiful awful thing that ever happened to me. I told them to stay strong in their faith. I thanked God for giving me such grace and strength. I comforted Andy's family, Katie and her Mom and their family. I comforted my family. I comforted them all. Comforting others gave me purpose and distraction from my own needs.. I lost my children in all of it. I was surrounded by people for hours and I lost sight of their needs. I heard they were being helped. I could not leave my post to check.

My friends bought food. They set it all up at my house. They served it. They cleaned it up. They directed us all back to the funeral home for the evening viewing where we would repeat it all. I did all I had to do, all I was supposed to do.

At the end of the evening, the people left us alone to say goodbye. My tired family cleaned up what they could carry and took some things to the cars. But, Katie. 19-year-old Katie. She didn't pick things up or gather her bag. She just stood at the casket staring. She would not move her feet in a final show of defiance in the name of her Dad. Katie is Andy's only child. He gave her as many of his attributes as he could. He taught her many life lessons, as all parents try to do. He also taught her to be tough. He taught her to push back and to be stubborn. He taught her that these were admirable qualities. It's just that they couldn't serve her here. No amount of "standing her ground" would bring him up out of the coffin to laugh and talk again. She whispered, "It looks like he could just get up." We sobbed near her. She knew, and we all knew that he could not. We also knew that if he could have, he would have done it for her. He always did anything for her. Maybe that's why she stood there waiting for so long.

It was painful to watch and wait with her. It was hard to even look at her. I had to look away, at my feet, even looking into the casket was easier than facing this confused and complicated step-daughter. Her mom tried to coax her away. Her boyfriend tried. Her best friend tried. The funeral director cleared his throat from the back of the room. They dimmed the lights in the nearby rooms. Still Katie stood her ground.

I walked up beside her and held her hand, another person who felt the great pain she was feeling. I whispered quietly as I looked at Andy's body about how he looked asleep and so beautiful even in death. Then I reminded her, and possibly myself along with her, that her Dad wasn't in there. I told her that we already said goodbye to her Dad two days ago. He heard us. We said what we wanted to say. I reminded her that she didn't have to say goodbye to the body in the coffin. She said something about wanting to remember his face, wanting to look at him as long as she could. Finally, she agreed to leave. Quietly, she turned away and came to the parking lot. It was beautiful, and it was awful.

Weeks later when I was driving alone in Andy's car, "I'll Follow the Sun" came on the radio. I cried as I listened to the lyrics about friendship and loss and realized they were meant for me to hold onto.

2

MEETING ANDY

I t was right that we should part to a song about friendship. We were married, but we were friends first. Andy and I were introduced briefly at the summer faculty meeting before the start of school in 2001. We were both high school teachers at Faith Academy Christian school on Long Island. I taught English; Andy taught social studies.

The next time we met, a few weeks later, I had both of my little children with me. My daughter, Corinne, was only three years old then. My son, Matthew, was six. I was tying the shoes of the younger one as I redirected the teasing of the older one in the echoing lobby of our school as Andy and I chatted for a moment about the kids and how I was raising them on my own after being separated from their father. Andy said he was also a single parent, divorced with one teen-aged daughter. I didn't share all the details with Andy then, but at the time, my two kids and I had moved out of our family home and were living in one bedroom of my parents' modest ranch. It was a big change for us, a hard time in my life. I was very thin, unhealthy, overwhelmed, and confused. Conversation with Andy was lighter than all that, though. We liked each other, but we were having a friendly colleague exchange only. Nothing more.

After that, we saw each other every school day, but we didn't interact much. I was completely absorbed with a long, angry legal battle, and he was just Mr. D'Angelo, the social studies teacher across the hall.

As time passed, I did get comfortable enough to visit Andy's classroom to hear a quick joke, a blurb of current events from his daily paper or crossword, something that would distract me from my divorce. He came to my room, too, for chocolate chip cookies – something I always have hidden in the bottom drawer of my desk and something I truly never share easily. We didn't fall in love then either, though.

A year passed this way. Another school year started. Andy was more relaxed as a teacher among the students and among the faculty in that second year, and I had begun to heal from my divorce. I taught first grade that year, while Andy remained in the high school wing. This meant that our classrooms were no longer in the same hallway, so we didn't get to chat in the morning. Instead, our lunch breaks coincided, though, and that's how we got to know each other better. We sat together on most days while we ate lunch. I fully enjoyed his company, over my peanut butter and jelly or occasional Kentucky Fried Chicken. I trusted his judgment and laughed at his wit. We talked about politics and history and music and religion. It was purely a co-worker relationship, as far as we were concerned, but people around us, especially speculating students of ours, got the idea that there would be something more.

I spent that year announcing that all I wanted to do was put a tremendous emphasis on *my God and my kids*. I made that declaration often so that I could ground myself, maybe. I wasn't planing to date. I was trying to get closer to God, to teach my children about His love, to learn about the one true relationship that would never let them down, the one they could have with God if they wanted. I met new people at Faith Academy, some happily married, some widowed, some fatherless, some divorced, who had learned the valuable lesson to put God first. They lived joyful, peaceful lives. They were healthy. My life, in contrast, was full of upset. I knew that I had strayed too far from my spiritual upbringing. I knew that the way back to joy was through God. Teaching a third year in a Christian school where my children heard Bible lessons every morning, where every class period started with bowed heads and a word of prayer and where others were around me on this same journey was no accident. I was meant to be working in this God-filled environment during those hard days of my life. I was meant to be involved with a principal and a faculty that loved God and counted their blessings and turned to Him first in times of trouble. Andy was putting his attention and energy into his mid-life career change. As a second-year teacher, he was knee-deep in lesson planning and grading rubrics. Neither of us were planning on nurturing a new relationship.

God set me up to make the most of that declaration to focus on *my God and my kids.* Working in a Christian school meant that every facet of my workday involved God. Every lesson, every book, every bulletin board was God-centered. My work relationships were with people of God. My children made friends with kids from families that loved God. Our weekends in church and volunteer time during the week involved our church and ministry opportunities, too.

Every morning, our faculty gathered in the sanctuary of our school building to pray. Students and classrooms and bus duty would wait until we first consulted with the Lord. We spent a few minutes in quiet prayer individually before coming together to pray as a whole. The teachers and administrators held hands in the quiet and called on God to direct our lessons and our words and actions. We asked God to keep angels around our building to protect us through the day. We thanked God for all that we had been given. I think the more mature in spirit were certainly listening for God to answer them as we prayed. I wasn't listening, though. I just didn't know how. I was grateful to be a part of this prayer time at work, but I didn't know how much I didn't know.

I was used to listening to my own worries and fears, and they muffled out the sound of God. I was only just learning to hear God's voice, to distinguish His voice from the sounds of fear or doubt or confusion. It was during this time of learning to listen for God's voice that I noticed something wrong with Andy. There wasn't a visible way to see a problem; I just *felt* that something was wrong.

On that particular day, I hadn't been praying. I hadn't been searching for an answer about Andy's health or questioning him on how he had been feeling. Why would God speak to me when I didn't even know I was listening? Andy just walked into our faculty room while I was sitting down at the round table to eat my lunch; I looked up and felt sudden alarm. I *saw* something. I saw sickness. I felt pending doom. I was instantly afraid. I didn't want to know, but I felt I did know: Andy was very, very sick. How did I know? Did God tell me? Others in the Christian school said they could hear the voice of God. Was this what He sounded like?

Andy had confessed during one of our earlier lunch chats to being a diabetic, but could that explain what I *saw* on his face? I was so full of worry that I felt like crying. I could see sickness, alarming sickness. Couldn't everyone see it? He looked really bad. No, not his color exactly. No, not his expression. Not fatigue. He just didn't look right. I knew that. I *knew* in a way that I couldn't define. I just *knew*. I had a very sure feeling that couldn't be justified by any practical reasoning, and that made me nervous.

In my Mom's Christian family of eight siblings, intuition is talked about often. I've heard my aunts and uncles talk and wonder and even laugh about how they sense things before they happen, how they feel connected to one another in a non-physical way. To the world outside of faith, that notion would be referred to as psychic. Psychic knowledge is in conflict with my prayer life, my spiritual side, and God's Word. Isn't it? So, yeah, I laughed along with my family when they joked about intuition being witchy, but it made me very uncomfortable. Somehow I missed when they suggested that this intuition was from knowing God.   I never imagined it to be part of my faith.

I never talked about it at church or at the Christian School where Andy and I worked.   I didn't think any-one there would laugh along with me. Is it even funny? There was something too real about it. I thought that accepting that I felt this intuition, too, made *me* wear the witchy label that my aunts and uncles made jokes about, so I hid it from my friends of faith. (As a confes-sional aside, it turns out that my own cranky behavior has caused me to bear the witchy label at times anyway, but that's a different subject entirely.)

After working in this Christian environment for almost three years, I think God may have been pre-paring to show me more about Himself. I wondered, "What is this knowing feeling I have about Andy? We barely know one another, but I am consumed with worry for his life." I didn't reveal any of it to Andy; I just showed him my concern and went back to class that day. I didn't collect another co-worker and pray. I didn't even ask my own class to pray about this. I planned to just get back to work after my lunch. Of course, I could think of nothing else, though.

Once my workday ended and my first graders had boarded their buses, I went to my principal. That's when I found out the shocking news that Andy had left work early that day because of illness. Still I didn't ask anyone to pray with me. I didn't run to God for answers. Instead, I waited until I got home, and I asked my Mom.

My Mom raised me up in faith and to know God, but she does not feel comfortable running in church circles or talking much about God and faith. That kind of intimacy is rough for some of us. My mom is one of that set.

I explained to her then that I had a *pending doom* feeling like I'd never had it before. I told her that this time I was terribly worried about the social studies teacher, Mr. D'Angelo. To add a twist, this time, I was unable to stop praying. I walked and prayed. I washed dishes and prayed. I was driving and praying. Even though I'd never done that before, I couldn't stop praying for Andy. I still called him Mr. D'Angelo in my prayers to God. I'd never had an occasion to use his first name. I didn't even know it. My heart ached with a giant dose of compassion, and I didn't know why. I was feeling a heaviness in my spirit from Andy not being well.

My Mom's reaction was to gently tell me that she did understand what was happening to me. She said that when someone is on her mind like that coupled with pending doom it means that they will die. She didn't talk of prayer. She didn't talk of any other possibilities.

She said she was sorry, but he would die. I was heart-broken. I was mad at God for giving me compassion or insight or whatever it was. I was mad at my Mom for telling me she thought he would die. I didn't want to know this. It was awful to see him and feel that he could soon be gone. I kept praying anyway.

The next day I was again shocked to discover that Andy wasn't at school. I panicked. I rushed to the principal's office to see what happened and to explain to Mrs. Warren what I'd been experiencing. I wanted to know if she could explain this feeling that I needed to pray unceasingly. It felt odd to me. Mrs. Warren is a strong-willed, intelligent, bold and faith-filled wom-an of God. She listened to me. I knew I could go to her for Biblical answers without gobbledy-gook and "Christian-ese." I hoped that she wouldn't judge me for saying I knew there was something wrong before it even happened. I needed her to tell me straight.

Mrs. Warren said that she knew what I meant. She wasn't shocked or alarmed. She didn't say Andy would die. She told me that I had to keep on praying. She encouraged me and told me she believed that God had prompted me to pray, had given me the knowing. She said nothing of psychic ability.

So, *God* had blessed me with this ability? *God* could be the one who prompted the knowing? I had never been comfortable with my gift of knowing because I didn't realize that it could be from God. Now, I suddenly felt grateful for the blessing! God was teaching me about who He is and how He operates.

And He was teaching me that it isn't so special to have this 'gift.' Many others know they have it, too. I was learning that all of us can hear God. I might have always called it my *inner voice* until then because I believed in myself more than I believed in the unknown God, but I was beginning to see the benefit in allowing that voice to be part of my prayer life, to understand it to be God answering me. I was beginning to see that I needed to listen more than I talk when I pray. Praying became a practice in fine-tuning my listening so that I could hear God. It was then that I noticed the Lord was showing me things that I might not want to hear with wisdom I certainly did not have.

Lastly, Mrs. Warren told me that Andy had been admitted to the hospital for some testing on his heart. I had to catch my breath. This truly was serious then. She said he was stable and talked to her on the phone earlier. She told me which hospital he was in. I couldn't wait to get home so I could try to call him.

Once home, I held the phone in my hand nervously, steadying myself for a moment, imagining what I should say. I was planning to call a guy in the hospital that I barely knew. I didn't want to seem like some busy-body who just wanted to be involved or get inside information. This conversation had the potential to be pretty awkward. I dialed anyway. It rang many times, as hospital phones usually do. I imagined him fumbling for the phone as I disturbed his rest or a visit with a doctor or family member. Once I heard him pick up – and actually called him Mr. D'Angelo because I couldn't get the word *Andy* out – I felt a lot better. He seemed pleased to hear my voice; that put me at ease a little bit. I asked how he was feeling; he explained what had happened in a light tone. Even though I was embarrassed to admit it to him, I boldly said what I'd been feeling. I told him that I didn't understand it, but I was praying constantly for him. I expected a weird silence as he took that all in. I expected him to think I was just another whacky Christian. He didn't, though. He sounded pleased. He said that it was good that I had been praying. He was glad that I was obeying what I felt God told me to do.

He also told me in that first phone call that he had had a heart attack previously, now years in his past. He said that this time he had only had a blockage that the doctors cleared with angioplasty. He would be back to work soon. He thanked me for the prayers, urged me to keep praying, and we hung up.

I went back to work the following day, still in prayer. I went to the office and offered to forfeit my prep periods off to fill in as substitute for Andy's classes until he returned. Mrs. Warren was happy to have me fill in. It was also a great opportunity to instruct our students to pray for him, too.

Soon, Andy did return to work. He felt better. He looked better. I felt better, too. Pending doom went away.

3

LET'S STAY TOGETHER

After his second year at Faith Academy, Andy left to find another position that could pay the bills better than private school. The school year had already started, but he was asked to begin working at Shelter Island public school on October 1st, 2003. He gave notice at work and asked me out to dinner to celebrate.

We had become friends over that summer after one of our high school students was killed in a car accident. Neither of us had a significant other in our lives with whom we could to talk to about our feelings of grief. We were both devastated by this beloved student's sudden passing. Losing a student is not something either of us had experienced before. We needed the mutual compassion of another teacher. At the burial, Andy stood near me while I quietly wept beside this 18-year-old boy's casket draped with flowers. The scene was horrific. Our entire Christian school encircled Christopher's remaining family, his Mom and Dad standing strong and firm in their faith while they watched their son's coffin beside a mound of fresh dirt. It was among all that sadness that Andy reached out for a few seconds to touch my arm, to comfort me. I felt a wonderful peace come over me. It was a very meaningful moment, something that felt very right.

After Christopher's funeral passed, we talked almost every day. At first, we just talked to check on one another and to compare how the other teens had been reaching out and managing their own grief at such a young age, but eventually, it turned into laughing and sharing and longer conversations that threatened to interrupt the sleep we needed for work in the morning. Neither of us minded. Andy even declared that I could "wake him up any time I wanted." I liked that.

I didn't admit this to myself at the time, but I was already falling for Andy. Our friendship had blossomed. After spending many hours on the phone, I found him to be smart, funny, honest, kind, caring, and spiritual. I wasn't looking for a relationship, but I wanted to spend more time with him. I agreed to go out to dinner.

That night was perfect. Everything was as it should have been. I fell in love with him while holding his hand as he drove us down Sunrise Highway. We were singing in the car -- together, at first. Then, I stopped singing. That may seem inconsequential from the outside, but those who know me know how much I love to sing. I always sing. I sing in my classroom, in the car, in the shower, while cleaning. I don't have the kind of voice that fills a room, but I can carry a tune. On this night, I stopped singing to listen. I listened to Andy sing in the most amazing voice I'd ever heard. I was mesmerized and awe-struck and quickly falling in love. By the time he kissed me at the restaurant, it was all over. We had an incredible night dining on a patio outside at this shmancy restaurant on Shelter Island. I took a nap on the long ride home. It was a perfect date. Every year, we counted that September night as our anniversary. Any hot, end-of-summer night reminds me of how special I felt then.

It was fall, 2003. After spending the summer concentrating on improving his health, Andy had slimmed down, had been going to the gym, and had learned to eat right. He was feeling and looking wonderful. Add in a new love and a new job and he was on top of the world. As for me, my divorce was final by then and my two kids and I lived on our own in a cape near my parents. I was feeling relieved and relaxed to have a messy divorce behind us. I didn't have a lot of money, but I didn't have debt either. My kids were healthy and happy and lived in a peaceful home. All was well.

Al Green sang "Let's Stay Together" to us often when we first started dating. We heard it on the radio all over the dial. It quickly became our song. We both had been through disastrous, financially devastating break-ups in our pasts, complete with custody battles, police reports and mud-slinging. We both understood how important it was that we make this one simple pact: to stay together.

As we got to know each other better, I only fell deeper into love. Any disagreement we had felt like a terrible disaster. When you're really in love, even the small things feel big. It's because the thought of anything ruining that bliss is that much more important. We worked things out, though, one bump in the road at a time.

One of the bigger bumps that we encountered was when Andy broke his shoulder. He fell from a scaffold in my house, while doing me a favor painting a cathedral ceiling. He fell onto his left shoulder, breaking it in two places and dislocating it. His entire family was out of town when it happened. It was July, 2004. We had only been dating for ten months. I had to manage his care both in the hospital and out. It was then that I began learning the details of his health history.

Andy took many medications. He took meds to slow his heart rate, to lower his cholesterol, to lower his blood sugar and to lower his blood pressure. He had heart disease, two prior heart attacks, had five stents already placed in his right coronary artery and had type 2 diabetes. He was a bit overweight also, so he was on special diets to stay as healthy as possible.

At the hospital emergency room where I met up with Andy after his ambulance ride, I first comforted him, then called his family. I noticed that he had his arm taped and tied to an IV pole so that no one would bump into it or jostle it. Ambulance workers were kind enough to set him up this way and no one had untied it yet. When he moved at all, he screamed in pain, so none of us even stood on the left side of his bed to keep from hurting him. From what I understood, the hospital staff was preparing to pull hard on that left hand and arm so it was actually further away from the socket. This would snap it back into place. Under any circumstances, that would hurt a lot, but, carefully taken x-rays revealed that Andy's shoulder socket was shattered. The pain of the break caused by this fall from the scaffolding was excruciating already. I saw the doctors and orderlies and nurses gathering around him, gearing up to hold him down while they tried to put the shattered bones of his shoulder back into place. They looked at me knowingly as if to say, "Yup. It's going to be that bad." They gave him lots of pain meds in preparation, but didn't give him anesthesia. Then they asked me to wait in the hallway. As I left I saw them positioning themselves with the strongest men they had on staff to hold him down as they pulled on his arm. I got to the hall and paced and prayed and paced and prayed and paced and prayed. All I could pray was the same thing over and over: "*Lord, please, send him an angel. Send him an angel. Please, God. Send him an angel…*"

I peaked into the room through the window in the door. I saw they were putting a bag over his face to help him breathe. I panicked. I continued pacing and praying. A few minutes later, one of the men that had been holding him down came out to tell me that he'd done well. He said that he was okay and I could go in to see him. Once inside, the nurse revealed that Andy had stopped breathing and that he had needed to be resuscitated. I walked to Andy's side and looked at his face. He turned to me, still dopey with pain medication, and only said two words: "Hello, Angel."

Now, Andy had never before called me angel. He never called me angel again, either. I looked up at God and said, "*Oh, no, God. I didn't mean me!*" Apparently, God didn't hear that. God must have had it all worked out that I would handle this. Throughout his healing, his family left Andy's care to me. He had to stay with me and my kids because he couldn't drive. He couldn't afford to eat without any income or money. He had been planning to spend his time over the summer painting with his father and brother in their family-run business. He could barely move, so painting was out of the question. Without that, he didn't have an income. If it hadn't been for the grace of his landlord, he would have lost his apartment. They agreed to wait for the rent until he was able to work again. That proved to take months.

So, Andy became our house guest. My kids, now just six and nine, were learning huge lessons on giving and nurturing and compassion for others. Our summer was transformed. Days of swimming and camping and hiking and bike riding were traded in for doctor appointments and trips to the pharmacy. Andy was really hurting, unable to move his left side, bruised, purple skin from his neck to his thigh. He had to stay with us. We did have a spare room. It was certainly not convenient, but it was necessary.

Andy was taking pain medication, but even with that drowsiness he was sleeping only in small pockets, feeling pain through a groggy head, unable to get comfortable or to roll over or even sit up or lie down without assistance. He couldn't feel better in any position.

He couldn't sleep well. He was frustrated by it all and irritable.

I felt helpless. I opened medicine bottles. I brought cold drinks. I rearranged pillows to sit him up, brought meals and helped him to eat them, but there was little I could do to speed along the healing process. Doctors said that it would just take time. He needed to rest.

Slowly, he did get well, eventually getting into surgery and then into a physical therapy routine that helped him regain mobility, but that took months. On his first night staying over, it was hard to see our way to healing. Sometimes brokenness and a feeling of helplessness besides leaves us no where else to turn but to prayer. That's all I could do. As Andy tried to sleep, I stayed beside him and I prayed. I whispered to God about bringing him peaceful sleep and about easing his pain and his worry about money and bills. I asked God to heal him quickly. Then, I waited. I touched Andy gently while I prayed. What happened next was overwhelming.

From that peaceful place of prayer and calm next to a now-sleeping Andy, I suddenly felt overwhelmed with grief and sorrow and extreme compassion. I started to weep and then sob and then eventually my breathing changed until I was actually crying, and not quietly. I couldn't understand why I was so upset, until I woke Andy up and started to talk it through. I blurted out, "I'm so sorry. I'm so sorry, Andy. I'm so sorry. I feel that God has given me knowledge that I don't want, but I have to tell you." He didn't interrupt me. He trusted me. He knew that I had been praying and that I had gotten an answer from God. He tried to soothe me. He touched my hair and looked at me as he waited for the rest.

"I'm so sorry," I repeated. "You are going to have a lot of pain. A lot of pain. I mean a lot of pain! *This* is painful and awful and seems terrible, but this is nothing like what is to come. I feel very strongly that you are just beginning down a very painful road. You are going to suffer," I cried. The emotion of it was taking me over. I couldn't bear to think of how awful Andy's suffering would be. I knew it would be very bad. "Oh" I caught my breath and put my hand to my mouth as the rest of it was revealed to me. "It's not only you. We both will suffer, but you will suffer physically. It's not me that will suffer physically. It's just you. I won't feel the pain. It's just you." I gasped for a deep breath here, hot tears on my face. "I will feel it all emotionally. I will stay by you and watch you suffer, and I will feel great emotional pain, great emotional pain. I will watch you suffer. Andy, I'm so sorry. It's true. I'm so sorry."

I cried next to Andy then, sobbing and completely exhausted from the power of this truth. I knew that

God had revealed something to us. It was sad, and it was true.

I felt terrible because I felt like I should be comforting him with words of encouragement and hope. I felt like I should be easing his worries and pain, but I could not hold back this awful truth from him about his life. I knew he would suffer great physical pain. I knew that, though this accident was extremely painful, there would be much greater pain ahead in his future. I *knew* this at that moment. I *knew* this. No amount of wanting it not to be true could push it away. It was true.

In that, I felt that we would be together. I felt that we would suffer together, but he would suffer physically, and I would suffer emotionally because I would be beside him. I just cried with him that night.

When I try to explain the fullness of the emotion from that moment of prayer, I am drawn to the memory of standing by Andy's coffin. The feeling is the same. That's how I felt. Overwhelming sadness. Bad news that punched me in the stomach. Sudden, unfixable and true grief.

Thinking back on this now, I see how much suffering we both had to endure and I see how God showed this to me beforehand to give me a choice. I did know. I had a full glimpse into our future.

Over the next weeks and months I thought of this often. Can I accept that this relationship will cause me pain and anguish? Is it worth it to keep putting myself into it? Is it worth it to give this much? Does it really feel that right? Are we really supposed to be together?

I called my best friend in California. Kerry moved there when we were just teenagers, but we maintained the closest of friendships. She is my confidant, my touchstone, my best friend. She knows how much I went through in my divorce. She stayed up with me through those nights in my past of crying and confusion and anger and jealousy. She listened and consoled me. She sent me flowers and cards and sweet little gifts to cheer me up on those days when I felt unloved. We haven't gotten a chance to bridge the physical distance between the east and west coast as often as we would like, but we are true friends to one another. She knows me, and she surely wants me to be happy.

I remember telling her that I could not get married to Andy. I thought I'd made a decision, and I announced it to her triumphantly. Wouldn't it be okay to stay dating? I told her that I loved him, that I never felt loved like this before, that we were very compatible and that she just had to meet him. He was funny, and smart, and very good to me. He was affectionate and thoughtful, and my kids loved him. She asked, "So, why aren't you going to get married then?"

I didn't have much of an answer except to say that I didn't want to be hurt. I already felt that the Lord told me I would lose him. "I'd be setting myself up to be a widow," was my answer. She knew I felt Andy wouldn't live long. I knew that.

Through the phone, I could hear her sigh. Then she paused a moment and said, "But wouldn't you rather be his wife when that happens? Do you want to just be his girlfriend? Do you think that the pain of losing him will be less if you aren't married?" She waited for my answer, but I had none. Then she added, "You already love him, Cath. You can't go back now. Married or unmarried, losing him would be devastating."

Though Kerry and I are both strong-willed, opinionated women who are comfortable enough with one another to speak our minds when we disagree, I had no argument for that. She was right. I was already in love. I was already set up for pain if I had to lose Andy. Agreeing to marry him wouldn't change that at all.

That conversation happened in the winter months on a Long Island drive through snow. Andy and I were married a few months later on May 27th, 2005.

4

LISTENING TO THE HOLY SPIRIT

I did know that I was setting myself up to be a widow. I'm not psychic. I'm not witchy. I just knew. It has taken me a long time of study and a long time of asking God to unravel it all, but I get it now. What I experienced that day was revelation from the Holy Spirit.

I haven't always discussed my personal faith and my relationship to God in such an open, honest way. Let me backtrack a little bit to help explain how I've gotten such boldness.

I was taught to pray as a girl. I cannot remember when I did not have a prayer life. What I mean by that is that I fell asleep each night talking to God about the mistakes I'd made, thanking Him for the good things in my life, and asking Him for what I thought were fair requests. That was the extent of the relationship. I knew He was there. I learned, like all good Protestants do, that I should not allow ritual or other people claiming to be devout to interfere with my personal relationship with God. I believed in the Father, the Son and the Holy Ghost, but I really had no idea about the Holy Ghost. I knew He was one of the trinity, but I'd never experienced Him personally or even known that I'd missed something.

So, in 2004, when Andy fell and broke his shoulder, I had very little understanding of how God worked in my life. I knew I had a relationship with a God who loved me. I tried to obey the Commandments laid out in the bible, but accepted the fact that my sins needed the grace that Jesus' sacrifice on the cross had offered. I attended church three times a week to learn more about Him and to feel closer to Him. I trusted God because He had proven Himself in dark days to walk beside me and carry me through where I knew I could never have walked alone. Yet, I was lost when it came to learning of the Holy Spirit. I was inquisitive, but I felt like I couldn't ever get to the bottom of it. I prayed for an increase in faith and for revelation. Revelation didn't come through lightning bolts or loud voices. Instead, it came in slow and well-timed experiences. I am still a student.

It is not a simple task to learn to listen to the voice of the Holy Spirit. In fact, for most of my life, I've been denying that it is possible at all. I could believe that if we prayed with a question, God could answer us in some way just after we left prayer. I believed that a sign could come, like a song on the radio, a commercial on TV, or unexpected contact with an old friend. I believed these coincidences were not coincidences. I believed that God might choose to give us divine appointments with people who could be like angels in our lives. That makes sense, too. These were acceptable ways for God to communicate with me. I had God all wrapped up in a neat little package that didn't seem too supernatural, but just different enough to be God and not only my imagination. Actually *hearing voices* would be schizophrenic; so getting signs and confirmations would be fine.

However, we do serve a limitless God. His communication with me did not stay in that neat little package.

As I searched and prayed and sang to God for direction and guidance and love, I began to hear my own voice louder. You must know what I mean: we have an internal *voice* of our own that speaks to us. With that in mind then, the best way for me to describe communication with God (Holy Spirit) is for me to tell you that that inner *voice* got louder.

At first, I really thought that I just had wild ideas. I would be at war with my inner voice. I would get an idea to do something that made me uncomfortable. Why would I do that to myself? I'll give you a few examples.

I remember standing in chapel with my high school students at the Christian school on a Wednesday morning. The chapel service began with praise and worship music and low lighting to allow the kids to invite the Holy Spirit with less fear of peer ridicule. Some kids stood around with their hands in their pockets, but others really prayed or meditated or listened for God's voice. What did I do? Remember, I love to sing. The words were up on a screen, so I stood with my class and really sang out to the Lord. This was a time for *students* to get closer to God, so, although teachers were also brought into the presence of God, we were supposed to behave in a more reserved manner so we could remain in a position of supervision. On one Wednesday, though, God had other ideas.

Instead of just singing I was standing there and feeling the urge to go stand up at the altar to sing to the Lord. I felt the urge to fall on my knees in the aisle and continue to praise God from there. I immediately dismissed it. I tried to sweep the idea from my head because I was sure I had the idea myself. This *idea* of mine would not let me alone, though. I didn't want to go. I wanted to stay comfortably in my place in that row of chairs in our chapel. Does God really need me to walk to the front of the room to pray and sing? *"God? Is that what you want? Help me to move if that is Your will."*

My feet felt cemented to the floor by my intellect; then my heart put my feet into motion. The rest just happened. Once I took that very first step – actually, it's less than that -- once I made the decision to move a fraction of an inch in the direction toward the altar, my feet took off by themselves. My heart beat too fast. I started sweating. My mouth went dry. I was trembling. These physical responses are all fear reactions for me, but I *went up anyway*. I stood at the altar facing forward, loving God, terrified, but feeling His approval for my obedience.

Other times I knelt there. I took these brave steps; and when I got there, I felt like God was pleased with me. It was a simple act of obedience and worship to a God I already knew I loved. It was odd for me to make the move. I worried what others were thinking. I worried that I might be laughed at or ridiculed. Maybe I was, but I *went anyway*.

As an inquisitive student of spirituality, I went back to the English classroom and asked my students how it felt when *they* were called to the altar. The students went up to the altar to pray all the time. They admitted to feeling the same sort of prompting to move, the same resistance to the attention, and then usually, the same surrender and calm. I know it may seem strange to go to teenagers with questions on God and communication with Him, but I had my reasons for this, too. Firstly, I had a relationship with these students where I could expect honesty in this area. Secondly, these were largely teens who had grown up learning about the Holy Spirit. They came from families whose parents had raised them up in the church. Though these ideas were new and foreign to me, they were not new at all to these kids. Answering a call from the Holy Spirit was something they understood better than I did. I don't mean to say that they had arrived or that they had all of the answers. On the contrary, they were searching, too. It's just that sharing these experiences helped us all to understand God better. It was good to hear the ideas outside of my own head, too.

Teenagers can be very reserved and overly concerned about saving face before others. They, by definition, are moved by the presumed thoughts and actions of their peers, yet these kids were different. They had had experiences together since preschool that set them apart form other teens. They had learned about the voice of God as a family of students. They had learned together that they were never alone. They knew that God was always with them. They may not have been able to overcome all social pressures, but in a small setting, there were opportunities to let their guard down enough to discuss the Holy Spirit. I learned a lot on those days, and here they thought *I* was the teacher.

God kept at it, too. He didn't just teach me things in church and in chapel services. He showed me that my inner voice was really His Holy Spirit residing right where I had asked for Him to be when I was younger: in my heart. I really did have a guide, a comforter, a counselor. Once I started listening, I found blessing after blessing in it.

I began to hear more often from the Holy Spirit. I would pray for answers or cry to God, as always, but my praying became a two-way street. I felt a communication with God, not just a one-way request line. Prayer became a source of comfort. No longer did I just find a release when I spoke out my troubles to God. In other words, I didn't just feel better based on having an emotional outlet. How then would prayer be different from talking to my best friend on the phone? I had found a real *friend* in God, my Creator, who knew me better than an earthly friend. I could pray, and I could listen. It was amazing and a great relief. It didn't happen right away, though.

Over time, I learned that I didn't need to designate a block of time for prayer. I still struggle with that. I don't have a chunk of time to devote to prayer. It's such an embarrassment to admit that, but it is true. I always mean to find time to go into my 'prayer closet' daily. Wouldn't that be great? To find an hour each day with no interruptions? To forget about the dishes and the laundry and the bills that need attention? To take the phone off the hook? To turn off my cell so there won't even be a text? To throw the dog and cat outside to fend for themselves? Nope. Not me. I am truly envious of those women around me who schedule their time so well that they pray in a regimented and always available time slot. I want to be like them. I just know that their socks are always paired up, and they never forget field trip permission slips on the counter or what time the dentist appointment is. I'm not like that, though. I really want to be, but, as of yet, I'm not.

So, I pray differently. As a full-time teacher and single mom, I am in the car a lot. I pray while I'm driving. I switch off the radio, and I talk to God. Sometimes I pray out loud. Other times I just think my prayers. I don't have a lot of time, so I make it quick. There are times that I have shouted out to God that I am confused or that I am scared or that I am overwhelmed. I ask Him for direction and strength and courage. I tell God that I love Him. I tell Him how grateful I am for being loved by Him. I thank Him for feeling loved. I count my blessings. I ask God to watch over my children or to help me through another day. I can quickly ask God, "*What do I do now?*" I usually hear back from God now, too.

What I used to consider my *inner voice*, is now understood to be the voice of God. I'm learning to listen better. I am able to discern God's voice from my own more and more. In quick, on-the-fly conversations with God, I have gotten answers to prayer, found understanding, or been given peace.

Sometimes, I've gotten wild ideas that I have told God were just stupid, too. I guess I was sure that God wouldn't say what I thought I'd heard. I've found myself laughing later on when I realize that I am arguing with my Creator!

"Okay, clay, be quiet." Naturally, the Potter does not take direction from the clay. I guess I just foolishly thought I knew better.

Another example of how God taught me to follow His voice and discern it from my own involves an average Sunday service in my home church. I was sitting on the left side of the church in about the fifth or sixth row back. I felt prompted to look up during the sermon. I saw an older woman sitting in the front row on the right side. That was nothing new. She sat there every Sunday. I didn't know her name. I didn't know her story. I didn't know anything about her except that she sat there every Sunday with a smile on her face as she listened to our pastor.

I know that in some churches, people move around or even talk during the sermon, but in this church we did not. It was uncommon for someone to leave the room during a sermon for a trip to the restroom, etc. Those that had little children in the nursery knew to sit toward the back in case they wanted to check on their babies. I didn't usually get up for anything during church, but on this day, I felt God telling me to stand up in the middle of the sermon, to pick up my Bible and my purse and my notebook and pen and go sit in the empty seat next to her. I felt like God was urging me to get up. I couldn't even listen anymore to the pastor. I had no idea what he was saying. I was trying to stay focussed on not getting up and moving my seat. I wanted to stay there and fight the urge to get up because I feared that it was just my own inner voice. I feared that I was wrong and that God wasn't asking me to move at all. Why would God ask such a silly thing? It must be me because God wouldn't want to interrupt the whole church service. He wouldn't want me to be such an attention-grabber on a Sunday morning. I reasoned that I must want attention.

Unfortunately, it was too late. I was now so concentrated on not moving that I wasn't even hearing my pastor. So, I gathered my things as quietly as I could manage, and I walked right down the center aisle and into the first row. I smiled nervously as I plopped myself and my disorganized things onto the chair next to the sweet woman of the first row. As I sat, she held my hand.

I went back to listening and taking notes as is my usual behavior on Sunday mornings. When the service ended, I turned to her with an apology on my lips. "I don't know why I moved this morning. I hope I didn't disturb you too much. I just felt really led to walk up here and sit beside you." She put her very old hand over mine and calmed my chatter. She said, "What is your name?" I told her that my name is Catherine.

At that, her eyes misted over. She seemed to have a lump in her throat as her mouth trembled before saying, "My daughter's name was Catherine. I lost her some time ago. I was just praying to God about how much I miss her. I was wishing Catherine were here beside me, and here *you* are. God answers prayer."

I could barely speak to her. I'm sure that I asked her name, but I don't even remember it now. She thanked me as we left the church. I remember leaving the parking lot and feeling sorry that it took me so long to respond to the call of the Holy Spirit. Why had I doubted? I asked God for forgiveness.

There was another time that I felt the Lord was teaching me how to listen in a similar way.

Unfortunately, I did not listen this time. I held my ground a little too long.

It was on another Sunday morning. I was again sitting in church. My usual seat was taken by visitors that day, so I sat somewhere else. Soon after I sat down, a young woman came and sat next to me. I didn't recognize her. She smiled and we introduced ourselves. I thought she was new to our church, but I wasn't sure. As the service went on, I noticed she didn't have a Bible in her lap. I considered reaching forward and opening one of the Bibles from the pew in front of us and offering it to her. I thought that would be a hospitable gesture, a Christ-like move. Then I heard it, felt it. I felt that God was disappointed in my idea, instead urging me to give her *my* Bible, not just to use, but to keep.

Now, I had a modest upbringing. I say at times that we were poor, but I surely knew others who had less than we had growing up. It may be a sorry excuse, but I just grew up stingy, and I think that growing up not having everything I asked for may have fueled that. I don't know. Maybe I'm just stingy. Either way, I sat there looking at my own personal bible. *My* Bible. The one with the great concordance in the back, the maps, the leather cover, the gilded pages, the words of Jesus highlighted in red, the notes from my own studies in the margin. How can I just hand her this Bible? What if she doesn't treat it like the treasure that it is? What if I hand her my Bible and she never opens it? What will I do then? I don't have the money to replace this Bible.

All of these excuses ran through my head, and I did not give her my Bible. All through the service, I felt that nagging voice telling me that I should give her the Bible. I kept considering it and dismissing it.

The service ended and the girl left right away. She did not linger and chat with anyone.

Moments later, as I victoriously gathered my Bible to walk out the door, feeling a little bit guilty, but mostly glad, the pastor's wife came and sat beside me. She had a big smile. "Did you get to talk to that girl who sat with you?" I told her that we had introduced ourselves and made small talk before the service, but that she ran away too fast afterward for me to get a chance to get to know her. Colleen's face drooped in disappointment, "Oh, darn. I was hoping to get to talk to her. I saw you with her, and someone else distracted me. She's my daughter's friend, and she's really searching for God, I think. She's having a hard time right now. I wish I had come over quicker. I wanted to give her a Bible."

I cried when I heard those words. I was so disobedient to my Father. Why hadn't I listened?

I know that these stories are not outrageous miracles of God's hand working. No one's life was at stake. Maybe no one is changed at all, except for me, but they are tiny ways that God answered my prayer to build faith. I continually asked God then -- and still ask now--to build my faith, to strengthen my faith. His answer to that is to show me in these little ways that He is with me. He is showing me that He loves me. He is teaching me how to listen.

5

MONDAY NIGHT

Andy and I were married in 2005 in an Assembly of God Church in Medford, New York. Two pastors presided over the ceremony: the pastor of the church, Pastor Anthony and our faithful friend and jokester, Pastor Lake, who knew us well from our days teaching at Faith Academy. He had been the Bible class teacher for the High School, the softball coach, and the gym teacher. Our wedding ceremony was beautiful. We had an itsy-bitsy reception, but we both felt that we had a superior ceremony, and that was what mattered most to us. The scripture, the music, the words spoken were perfect.

Following a long search for the perfect home to unite our two families, we settled into a house in Manorville, about 20 minutes east from our church. It was a 30-year-old house that was just on the cusp of needing repair in every area, but looked just good enough to get by for another couple of years with just new paint. The previous owners had taken exceptional care of it: gardens, greenhouse, in-ground pool, and huge yard. We knew by the time we were at the top of the stairs that we had found the right place. It was too expensive, but somehow the mortgage went through. We knew we were meant to be there. God had blessed us with this new home. We had a new place to start our life together as a family of five. We both felt really grateful that God had blessed us, so when Pastor Anthony announced that he was looking for hosts for in-home fellowship groups that October, we both felt called to volunteer our home and give back to the Lord. It was right that the house would be used to bless God back.

Each small group was meant to meet once a week for seven weeks. We were given copies of *The Purpose Driven Life* for each person joining in. We also got a teaching dvd that we could play to help us with our discussions each week. It all seemed a little bit too organized and neat and pre-planned, but we agreed.

We had a core group of five of us to start. We met on Monday Nights. We faithfully watched each week's dvd segment and made attempts at keeping discussion on the topic prescribed, but we more-often veered off that purpose-driven path, and that is where we really started to learn about our faith.

We dutifully finished the mandatory seven weeks of the book discussion, and then all agreed that we certainly were not done meeting. We were building friendships that had begun in the social and in the instructional, and had now moved on to the spiritual. Our discussions could land on politics or economics or history, but we had now begun relating that to God and the Bible. Andy being a history teacher, and others in attendance being very politically aware and educated set us up for truly applying what God's Word teaches us. We batted around ideas of truly loving our neighbor as ourself and how that related to our work lives and to our job choices and to the way we raised our children. We had examples each week of ways in which we'd seen God working through the people we encountered and ways that we were sure were in opposition to God's Word. We examined and re-examined the life of Jesus and his teachings. We meditated on the sacrifice at the cross. We encouraged one another to trust God and to take steps out in faith that we wouldn't have otherwise taken.

Monday Night, as we came to call it, was sometimes a Bible study, sometimes a therapy session, sometimes a social group, sometimes a prayer group, but always we came away better on Tuesday morning for having met once again. Monday Nights have taken many shapes. We have always been open-minded and accepting of new ideas and voices and questions. We have had nights of pure praise and worship where we have music filling the house. My children have often fallen asleep upstairs on these school-night Mondays to the sounds of praise music. Other nights are all social chatter and catching up with one another. At first I used to feel that we were cheated out of our Monday Night experience when we just talked all night, but we've all come to understand that the social nights are necessary, too. We have to trust one another in a forum like this one. Getting to know each other well and really building trust are critical in the face of trial or when considering deep moments of honest prayer.

There are gripe nights, too, where someone is venting about a work-related problem or a family issue. There are actual Bible study nights or book talk nights, too. We even had a few nights on meditation. We all had an unspoken agreement, though, that Monday night was a safe place for us to talk openly, to step out in faith without ridicule, to support one another first in love. Monday nights have been beautiful. We never know who will walk through the door. It can be all 'regulars', or it may be fresh faces. It's usually a combination of these. Anyone who has been involved in a small group like this knows. It's a unique experience. It's a commitment to one another.

Monday Night always changes, though. We never know who will walk through the front door. We never know how we are called to know them, help them, or maybe how they are called to help us. We greet new-comers with open arms and share our Monday Night snacks and cups of tea with them. Sometimes I even share chocolate chip cookies.

I knew even then that Monday Night was about lov-ing each other. I knew that we were together and what that really meant. We could trust one another to be loved and supported in our walk. We could take little risks in how we praised God or share how God had made His presence known during our week. We got comfortable in this. Now, I see that God was strength-ening us for what was ahead. He had given us the gift of each other. We never expected that comfort and love and trust to be tested, but in August of 2007, it was tested.

Over that summer, Andy needed another shoulder surgery to repair that prior break and dislocation from back when we were dating. The surgery itself went well, but six days later, we rushed him to the hospi-tal with chest pain. Andy was having a heart attack! The hospital that we took him to was unable to clear the blockage. He was in terrible pain that they could not relieve. They agreed to transport him to a local university hospital by ambulance. There they would admit him to the cath lab and perform angioplasty to clear the blockage with placement of a stent. I was told to say goodbye to my husband before he boarded that ambulance. We did not expect to see each other again.

I drove out of that hospital and picked up my cell phone. I made two calls. I called my mother to make sure my children were cared for. Then, I called Judi, a regular on Monday Nights.

Judi must have made a call or two. Within an hour, the hospital waiting room was full of family members and Monday Night friends.

Andy came through the procedure very well. He needed to stay a few days and follow-up with rest and then cardiac rehab, but he was okay. When our pastor came in, he perked up. He realized how much love was surrounding him. It was beautiful.

So, this was the first drill of the emergency system that Monday Night turned out to have. There would be many times over the next six months that this system would be put into use. Each time support was needed (financial, spiritual, emotional, practical) our Monday Night family met the challenge with joy. Our leaves were raked in the fall. Meals were supplied for our family when we were unable. Gifts arrived at Christmas. The kids were cared for. Our pets were cared for. Money was dropped off anonymously. Our mailbox was daily full of little (and some big) checks to help us out. We can point to the kindness and love of our Monday Night family for all of that. Somehow, they organized people to help us. They understood our needs without our voicing them. They just loved us. They felt love. They acted in love. It was the spirit of Monday Night in action. There was no glory. There was no discussion or intricate plan. It was just a time to love.

The second great trial we experienced in this series of tests for Monday Night happened a few weeks later. Andy had been recovering from his heart attack, getting more active daily. I went in for a routine mammogram in late October in the morning before work. The doctors at the breast center didn't let me leave, though, because they wanted an immediate biopsy of an area in question. On Long Island, we battle breast cancer very seriously. We live in an area with a very inflated rate of deaths related to breast cancer. Even though I would be missing work on a day that I simply could not, the doctor insisted that I stay until they determined whether I had something to worry about.

I stayed. They ran more tests: mammogram and ultrasound and eventually biopsy. They determined that I needed to be seen by a surgeon. The cells in question were beginning to form in a stellar pattern indicating a pre-cancerous condition. They insisted that I consider surgery as soon as possible.

Andy and I left the breast center that day in silence. I was in pain, rattled by the news that I needed surgery on what was likely a cancerous spot on my breast. Cancer. Cancer? Wow. My grandmother had breast cancer early in her life, a radical mastectomy, radiation treatments that damaged her lungs permanently. Was I really going to follow down that road? I had to call work. I had to call my Mom. I had to find a surgeon. I had to take more days off to recover. What kind of surgery would this be? Would I need chemotherapy afterwards? Who would take care of me? Andy was still recovering from his heart attack. The kids would need care, too. My mind raced. I thought I'd call my Mom and ask her to come stay with me for a week or so. The ideas spun out of control. I was in a panic now.

I couldn't cry. I couldn't let me kids see how upset I was. I didn't want them to worry. I decided not to frighten our children with the details, choosing instead to wait until I had more solid information, but I did call on my Monday Night friends to pray for me.

Unfortunately, Andy also had tests done that day. We were trying to determine the cause for his sudden jaundice. We didn't think it was related to his recovery from the heart attack. We thought maybe one of his medications wasn't working correctly. We were not as alarmed by his yellow skin color as we should have been.

Similar to an Alfred Hitchcock movie where the enemy is not the enemy you expect or the fate you fear is not the one the viewer should have been fearing, we were not worried about the real enemy to come. We were worried about Andy's cardiac health. We were now also worried about my battle with breast cancer. We were completely blind-sided when we learned that Andy's jaundice was being caused by a tumor on his pancreas. On Halloween of 2007, we got the shocking results of an inoperable condition that would presumably end in his death.

By this time when Andy was diagnosed with cancer in 2007, Monday Night had had many, many experiences with the Lord and with the Holy Spirit that had fully changed us as a group and as individuals. We loved each other. We trusted each other. We loved God together, and we built each other up in faith as we felt we were called to do, like loving one another will naturally lead to. Our faith had reached incredible heights. Not even one of us would consider missing our fellowship time together. It fed us before another week of the world.

More than in any other area, I believe our prayer lives changed the most. We learned to pray in the Spirit. We learned to call on the Holy Spirit, to lay hands on one another for healing, deep healing of our bodies and our minds. We learned to listen to the voice of God in our prayers. We learned not to act until we were led to act and we heard from God in prayer. We studied the Bible, but more than the scripture, God taught us about His ways and His love through the Holy Spirit. Monday Night was nothing short of supernatural then. We praised God in song, lifted His name in praise with a week's worth of faith reports, we reached out to give in missions, with money, with our time. We stepped out boldly in faith to do what we felt God leading us to do, to further His kingdom. We were really excited to call ourselves Christian, to have found God right there on the blue carpet in my living room. Looking back on it now, it is clear that God was building up our faith for the fight that was to come.

Andy's cancer diagnosis stopped us in our tracks. We paused for a while, quieted by it. Monday Night was confused. "How could God let this happen if we have been so faithful?" was surely in our hearts, but none of us spoke it out. Instead we spoke through pure and blind faith. We girded one another up. We held up each others' hands. We were intelligent people, who fully understood that pancreatic cancer is not curable. We all knew this. We knew that this diagnosis likely meant that Andy would die a quick and awful death, and be gone. We had no idea how to manage that. So, we called for a prayer vigil.

After Andy's condition was stable following the heart attack, I wrote an email to keep our friends and family informed of his condition. Further emails updated them. Monday Nighters were included in those emails.

6

HEART ATTACK AND ANDY'S RECOVERY

Date: August 29, 2007
Subject: Andy's recovery

Hi all,

I'm writing to let you know that Andy had a heart attack on Tuesday evening. He is now doing well, and the blockage is 100% cleared, but last night was tough.

His Dad took him to Riverhead hospital at around 4:30 in the afternoon when he complained of severe pain in the middle of his chest. We debated about taking the drive to Stony Brook University Hospital instead. We are glad we did go to the closer hospital. They were able to stabilize him and move him to Stony Brook in about an hour. They took him right to the

CATH lab that they have there. They put in two stents and cleared the blockage. They said the blockage was apparently 100% at Riverhead, and they were able to clear it with blood thinners (clot buster in the IV) to 95%. If they hadn't, he wouldn't have made it to Stony Brook at all.

Many of you already know that Andy had surgery 5 days earlier (on Thursday) to remove the screws in his shoulder from his break three years ago. That surgery apparently went well, but he is in a great deal of pain now from moving it so much in the cardiac care unit.

Let me take this opportunity to thank and praise God Almighty for sparing him once again. We know that God has a great plan for his life and needs him here to implement it. Please continue to pray for guidance for our family in the future. We don't understand the big picture here. Right now it seems like senseless pain and worry. Please help us in praying for a deeper understanding.

Also, I want to say, 'thank you' for all who have been in prayer for Andy's complete recovery. So many of you were able to come to the hospital to support me in a very difficult time. We really didn't know what last night's outcome would be. Thank you so much for coming to be with me for the waiting.

He is now smiling and talking about the great menu at the hospital! (Literally, the food he's ordering has been outrageous!...and all healthy!) We are expecting him home on Friday. The cardiologist isn't sure how long he will be out of work -- a few weeks at best. Please pray for Andy to have peace about that. He's already trying to figure out when he can get back into his classroom.

Forgive me for sending such an impersonal email message. I have been on the phone since I woke up at 5:30am. I simply can't reach all of you that way. I need to go be near him now. We both feel better that way.

:) Feel free to forward this message to others. Our contact info is below.

~Catherine D'Angelo

7

CARDIAC REHAB

Date: Friday, August 31, 2007
Subject: Cardiac Rehab

Hi all,

Thank you very much for your responses of love, support, prayers, and offers to help. I'm sorry that I haven't been able to personally speak to all of you. Email continues to be the best form of communication.

Andy is expected to come home from the hospital today. He has been told that he can do nothing for the next week but get up to use the bathroom. Apparently the first week is a crucial week of healing for the heart muscle.

Also, his shoulder and arm are very swollen. He is controlling the pain with ice packs and those (when-needed) pain meds, but he still can't move very well and needs help with tasks he could've otherwise handled.

Unfortunately, I am returning to work on Tuesday. I won't be home until 4pm on each day. We will need volunteers to bring him a heart healthy lunch and spend a few hours with him each afternoon...maybe from 12-2pm? I would like to set up a schedule for each day (Tuesday - Friday). Please let me know if you are available to take a day. He may need some support for the following weeks as well (Mondays through Fridays), but I'm most concerned about the first week.

After this week, he will return to the cardiologist. They will do an ultrasound of his heart (echocardio-gram) to determine how he's been healing. Then, they'll tell us how to proceed as far as a return date to work, resuming normal activity, etc.

Please call, visit, send emails, bring a Newsday, etc. He will need encouragement and support. As usual, he's having a hard time accepting restriction to his ac-tivity. A man feels best when he can do. It's difficult to keep him down for so long. Any help that you can provide is welcome. :) It's hard for us to act in humility and accept help from others, but we do need you. It's a time for humility.

What should we take from all of this? What lesson are we being given? So far, we have only the obvious: each day, each moment is a gift. Our lives are in God's hands. We need to follow the path that He has planned for us -- even when it seems contrary to the direction WE planed to go. We haven't figured out how to do that yet.....hahahahahahaaa....we're still praying, though. :)

Again, our contact info is below. Thank you, thank you, thank you.

~Catherine

8

D'ANGELO NEWS

Date: October 27, 2007
Subject: D'Angelo News

Hi all,

Here is another, impersonal, on-the-fly update form the D'Angelo house.

Andy's been in cardiac rehab for about six weeks now (that's supervised exercise three times per week). He had a stress test that showed good blood flow and no apparent trouble spots. He's supposed to start school on November 5th.

Unfortunately, fatigue started creeping in this week, and now he's very jaundiced. We've been to the doctor, had blood tests done, etc. His liver counts are high. They will have an answer on Monday, but they are speculating that he has hepatitis. We don't know if it's A, B, or C. We don't know how he could have gotten it or how they will treat him. We'll know more on Monday. Until then, he's tired and yellow. :(

On another note, I went for my annual mammogram. They found a new cyst and some architectural changes to the breast tissue. They had me come in again for some more tests and then had me stay so they could biopsy both areas immediately. As it turns out (though we read that 80% of architectural changes are cancerous) mine are benign!! (Good news.) Unfortunately, they still would like to remove that area of the breast and the cyst also. I'm currently looking for a surgeon. The cells are abnormal at this point, and they are concerned that they will turn into cancer. I'm sore and have been home from school for two days. I'm headed back to school Monday.

We're both emotionally drained. We know how you've been praying for us. Thank you all for all of your support. I'll write again when I know more.

~Catherine

ps. God's still in control! :) We don't always understand that, but we know it's true.

9

PRAYER VIGIL

Date: November 3, 2007
Subject: Prayer Vigil

To our wonderful family and friends,

I am sorry to tell you this in an email, but we have gotten a terrible medical report. On Thursday night, we got the results of Andy's CT scan. It shows a large tumor at the top of his pancreas. It's pressing on the bile duct and on the liver. He has been jaundiced since last week because of this. The tumor is interrupting his ability to get nutrition. It is presumed to be cancer. A biopsy has not yet been ordered. It seems that even if the tumor were benign, it would not be less life-threatening. We have also been told that the tumor is surrounding a major artery/vein that supplies the gastro-intestinal area. Yesterday a procedure was done at Mather hospital to open the bile duct with a stent. The procedure was a success and the jaundice should dissipate. However, there is no way to operate on the tumor. In other words, the doctors are not optimistic.

We are faith-filled Christians, however, and we refuse to believe that God would tear us apart so soon! We will not accept this bad report. We are in constant prayer and meditation. We are sad, but we are also strong and stubborn. We know how to fight and we are ready to put the fight toward this invasive thief of a tumor. Please stand in agreement with us.

We have turned our Monday Night into a prayer vigil. On Monday, November 5th, we will be meeting at 7pm to pray and pray and pray! Please be with us in person or just in prayer from where you are. We know that there is an incredible testimony on the other side of this ordeal. Won't it be amazing to see Andy standing and giving this testimony when he is well again? We are not delusional; we are just faithful! We are ready for battle. Come strengthen us.

We are planning to leave on an airplane to Philadelphia on Wednesday. We are going to one of the 'Cancer Treatment Centers of America' for three days. Please read about it through the link below. They will organize a treatment team for Andy based on his individual case that includes an oncologist, a surgeon, a gastroenterologist, a naturopath, a psychologist and a pastor. They will treat the whole patient: spiritually, physically, and emotionally. We can choose to execute the treatment plan in Philly or bring the plan home to Sloan Kettering. We haven't determined that.

We are looking forward to seeing you on Monday Night.

All are welcome

~Catherine

ps. As always, please forward this to anyone I might have missed.

10

JUST SHY

A ndy was a superior teacher and an excellent public speaker. He could address a crowd in a captivating way. He paced in front of his classroom with his hands clasped. He gestured in his full-blooded Italian way. He flashed that adorable, dimple-filled smile in just the right places. His humor kept it all interesting. His honesty was inspiring. He caught the attention of the listener. His students did very well on those stringent New York State Regents exams because they were so enthralled with him, so attentive to his every word. Well, let's be honest, teenagers are never attentive to *every* word, but they listened. They loved him. They respected him.

Years earlier, when Andy announced he would be leaving his position as Christian school teacher to move on to public school, his students wrote petitions to try to keep him. It was the only means they had at their disposal. They hoped that if enough of them wanted him to stay, the school might try to pay him more to keep him there. The petition was a beautiful gesture, but the school simply couldn't compete with the salaries of the public sector. So, he collected email addresses of students that wanted to stay in touch. He truly loved them, too, and wanted to remain in contact. He wanted to check on them and how they were doing. He wanted to bless them with his guidance and wisdom when they reached out for it. He wanted to keep them on track, make a difference in their lives. He knew that he already had. He had won their respect, and he felt it. He loved that feeling, and he knew that it came out of truth and genuine love for them. There was nothing phony about his caring about his job and his students. It was obvious.

Once he was teaching on Shelter Island, Andy worried that the connections made with public school kids wouldn't be the same. He soon learned that it wasn't just the heart of the Christian students in the easy-going, Christ-filled community of a Christian school that facilitated those great relationships. It was Christ in Andy that brought it all about. The kids could feel his love through his teaching and his outreach to them after hours. He was more to them than just a social studies teacher. I know this not just by their performance on state exams, but also because of the overwhelming outpouring of love shown by his students when he got sick.

In fact, when the Shelter Island School learned that Andy was sick and that they might lose him, they reached out constantly to support him. Giant oaktag cards held together with yarn and decorated with glitter came to the house with well-wishes and messages of love. Envelopes with money were hand-delivered to the house and when opened were found to be filled with single dollar bills, money very obviously collected by students who were likely giving up their lunch money to donate to the healing cause of their beloved Mr. D. Dances were held in his honor where more donations were collected. These donations helped us to get our house out of foreclosure. A school-wide project that now included the Middle School children, who weren't even old enough to have been students in his class yet, ended with one thousand paper cranes being folded for Andy. The intricate origame cranes in brightly colored paper and the hand-made cards and the daily mail that came with get-well wishes kept our house decorated with reminders of how much the students loved him.

The teachers collected money in his name, too. They sent Andy books and letters and emails and called often. They came out to our Monday Night prayer vigil and blessed us with their show of love. Together the teachers of the Shelter Island School signed a hand-made quilt with Sharpie marker so that he could be literally covered in the love that they had for him as he lay sick in his bed on those last days. Eventually, that quilt would rest on his coffin in the funeral home.

The superintendent of his district allowed a school bus filled with students to transport those kids on the hour-long ride out to Andy's wake. Imagine the love that overwhelmed us all to see a school bus outside of a funeral home where an entire student body had been shuttled to honor and respect Mr. D. one last time. It was very moving. To hear them speak was even more emotional. He was teaching them right up until this last minute, about leaving a lasting impression and about perseverance. He was teaching them about love and faith and goodness. They did learn those lessons, too, even if they can't be demonstrated with state exam scores.

Andy was special. Everyone who knew Andy truly did know that. Yes, he was my husband, so my word on this may not carry as much weight, but it is the truth. The evidence of his legacy shows that.

Now, to hear how Andy was an exceptional speaker who was able to be such an incredible influence on those who were privileged enough to be in his classroom and then to hear me tell you that Andy described himself as shy seems inconsistent. I know, but it is true. Andy explained that he had to force himself to get up and speak, that it didn't come naturally. For me, it was hard to imagine Andy as a quiet child who rarely spoke up in school or one that had anxiety over being called on by his teachers. He told me that it was with great effort that he overcame his shyness. I only saw lingering signs of that once in a while. I could only see it in his occasional introverted behavior. He used to say, "I don't like anyone. It's a great compliment that I spend so much time with you. I don't want to spend this much time with anyone else." I think that was an exaggeration aimed at making me feel special, but it had some truth in it. I was our social planner. I made arrangements for us to go to parties, have company over our house, or to visit with friends or family. Once in a social situation, he seemed happy enough. He mingled and chatted and smiled. He didn't pout and retreat. I guess this was just another way that we complemented one another.

As for me, I have never been described as shy. In fact, as a teacher, the shy child is the one I understand the least. I don't get it. I don't want to be alone. I love being around people. I love having company. I love talking to people. In fact, allow me to change that: I love talking! I talk to thin air if no one is there to listen. As a child, I talked to stuffed animals and I talked to adults who were tired of my chatter, I talked to bugs and worms that I found outside who I called my friends. I talked and talked all of the time. Naturally, I talked to God also. He was a consistent and captive audience. I got to know God to be the one who always listened. I always felt heard. That's a beautiful discovery for a young girl who might not have otherwise had an outlet.

So, as a couple, Andy and I had some adjustments to make. I continually wanted to be social. He truly enjoyed alone time. I wanted to talk on the phone, or to him all the time. He wanted to silently watch the Yankee game. I called him at work to talk on his breaks. I loved sharing my ideas and concerns with him throughout the day. My chatter drove him crazy at times; his silence was deafening to me.

I learned through my life that when times get tough, I need to draw on God and my friends. I call on my family. I call on my church family. These are the survival strategies I've come to rely on. Andy, on the other hand, did no such thing. In times of trouble or upset or just deep contemplation, he withdrew. He prayed alone, communed with God to find answers to his troubles. He wrote in his journal. He took a drive. He rarely picked up the phone to find answers. It seems to me, he preferred *having* the answers before he met up with others.

So, what happened when we were faced with these trials?

What happens when a couple who has opposite tendencies have a tragedy falling on their home? Do we retreat? Do we write? Do we as a couple agree to commune with God in prayer? Yes. We did. For one day, we did. I wallowed in my sorrow for one whole day. By the end of that day, though, I had abandoned all sense of alone-ness. I did not have any interest in keeping our upset private. I could not. I announced to Andy that we had to call his family and tell them the news he'd been holding in for nearly 24 hours. He cried. He didn't want to tell anyone. He didn't want to disappoint them.

I never saw Andy cry before for any reason. His shoulder shattered, he had financial distress, we had some disagreements, we had a beautifully moving wedding ceremony, his daughter left for college, we had to say goodbye in a hospital Emergency Room before he was transported to a cath lab during a heart attack, and even the news of his own terminal cancer: still no tears. He was stubborn, maybe, to not show that side of himself, but he couldn't hold back the tears once faced with sharing this news with his mother.

I only heard his side of the conversation. He told her the medical report. She immediately put it all together. She burst into tears and hung up the phone. No goodbye. No 'I love you'. She just hung up. He called her back twice, weeping all along. She wanted to cry. She would talk to him again later. Then, he called his Dad, his brother, his best friend, his employer.

I had a different way. I had started sending emails when Andy had the heart attack. I emailed our students, our fellow teachers, our bosses, our church family, our family, our friends. I sent mass emails meant originally to update the people that cared about us on doctor appointments and medical procedures and healing. I did not know that my "networking," as Andy called it, was anything more than just a convenient way for me to spread news. In the cases of my closest family and friends, I naturally made more personal phone calls, but the emails were a way to be sure that no one was missed.

Without sending those emails, I would have been on the phone constantly, and I never would have been able to reach everyone that needed to hear the news. It's not that I minded being on the phone, in fact, I was still on the phone all the time; I was just unable to stay in touch with everyone with phone calls. It was too time consuming. People understood that I could not physically do that. They would have preferred the phone call, but accepted the email. The emails gave me a way to give everyone the same information and to not let it get mixed up in the translation like a giant game of telephone.

That's how this all began. Instead of just writing my worries in a journal and chatting on the phone with my friends, I wrote the emails.

11

TELLING THE KIDS

After the adults in the family had been told, we knew we had the biggest hurdle to go over: the children. Matthew, 12, and Corinne 9, lived at home. They were out at school as they were on any old Friday. We decided we would talk to them after their school bus pulled up.

Katie, 19, was away in college. Katie meant everything to Andy. How could he tell her? His only daughter? What kind of news is that to get over the phone? Katie lived with us finally after a lifetime of divorced parents and turmoil in her living arrangements, where she chose to live with friends over family in search of stability and a healthy home. Finally, she got to settle in with her Dad in the home we made. She got to live with him, have her own bedroom, a normal life where, though there was financial strain, we weren't living in poverty and she could have her own space, a yard, a family. Children of divorce don't always get that luxury. There's often a heavy price that our children pay. This news would disrupt that newfound peace. This news would disrupt everything.

Andy lived for his daughter. He literally lived for her. There was a time in his life, at his lowest point, that he truly didn't want to live anymore. It was Katie needing him that made him reconsider his suicidal thoughts. It was God that showed him that truth.

On this November morning, Katie was away in her second year at college in Albany, New York, four hours away. We imagined her contentedly going through her day, her greatest difficulties being her next assignment due or scheduled exam, and what might happen when we disturbed all of that with devastating news about her Dad. I recalled that when I was in my first year of college, my grandmother passed away. I had been grateful to know months in advance that she was dying of emphysema, so that I could prepare, so that I could talk with her about it. My grandmother and I were not very close, but she did live in the house next door to me, and I did love her. Losing her wouldn't be easy. Watching her die would be painful for all of us, but there was a blessing in knowing it was coming, not being surprised by it. I imagined that, if given the choice, Katie would want to know everything.

He didn't call her right away. He kept putting it off. All day, he had excuses for not dialing her number. He thought the timing was bad. He thought she would be too upset. He wanted to know more before he called and worried her. He thought maybe he'd wait to tell her until after he met with doctors again, had more information about what this illness meant. We both knew that pancreatic cancer meant he was going to die. In Andy's own shouted words, "Pancreatic cancer??! That's a DEATH SENTENCE!!" We knew what his diagnosis meant. We thought of Michael Landon and how quickly he died. That had been the most publicized case of pancreatic cancer we'd heard about. We knew that Andy didn't have long. We hoped that science and medicine had made progress in recent years and had developed a new way to allow patients to live longer with this cancer, if not cure it altogether, but we were realistic. In talking to the kids, we wanted to give them hope and realism at the same time. We wanted them prepared for Andy's death while they hoped and prayed for him to live.

His call to Katie, as I remember, was honest, but not forthcoming. Andy left out the part about him having pancreatic cancer. He told her that he had a tumor on his pancreas. True. He told her that it was pressing on the common bile duct and that it was causing him to be jaundiced. True. He told her that the doctors would put in a stent to open up the duct in an outpatient procedure. True. He told her that the tumor couldn't be biopsied right now because he had recently had a heart attack, and it wouldn't be safe. There was no confirmation on whether the tumor was malignant. All true. However, he left out the part that, regardless of its malignancy, it was life threatening as it pressed on the bile duct. If his digestion were interrupted this way, he could not live. He left out that his doctors had already told him he had an inoperable tumor on his pancreas that would take his life. Instead, he spoke to her in light tones, asked her to come home for that weekend, and reasoned with me and with himself that he'd explain better in person. I understood. I thought that it would be best for him to be able to look at her and hug her during a conversation like that, too.

When Matthew and Corinne came home, they were surprised to see that I hadn't gone to work. They knew that this was my tenure year in the public schools and that I could not take any days off from work. They also knew that I had already been forced to take some time when I had had that bad mammogram. They dropped their backpacks and grabbed snacks and drinks. I told them that we all had to talk. I told them that they had to sit down at the kitchen counter with us. I guess that set them up for some bad news. I think back now and realize that they surely felt anxiety about me asking them to sit down and talk with us. Andy pacing in the adjoining dining room didn't help to set them at ease.

Corinne didn't want to sit down. She stayed near me as I dried my wet hands at the kitchen sink. I told them I had something I had to tell them. She interrupted me with a loud, "We already know. You have cancer, right?" I was stunned. Stunned that she knew it was cancer, sad that she carried this knowing through her school day, and sorry that I could only give her a moment of relief in telling her she was wrong. I corrected her, hugged her, and told her that it was Andy that had cancer. I told them the truth, in the gentlest way that I could, then I told them that we were meeting with new doctors and that we were praying to God for healing. I reminded them that we are people of faith. They said no more. They didn't cry. I made dinner.

The next day, November 2nd, Katie came home. We shuffled the younger kids around, and then the three of us went to the movies. Katie and Andy both love the Beatles. Andy fully admitted to brainwashing his little girl into loving the Beatles as he did. He was proud of that work. Andy was a tremendous Beatles fan. Knowing Andy meant learning about and appreciating the music of the Beatles. He could tell stories about each song's release, each purchase he made at the music store as a kid growing up listening. He could link Beatles music to lessons on culture and politics and war and peace and government and social commentary. He believed the music of the Beatles epitomized American cultural changes of that era, and he didn't love them just for that. He respected the individual musical abilities and talents of each of the Fab Four, and especially admired their song-writing. Andy loved music, was open-minded about new sounds, could critique or appreciate something that was just a fad, and recognize when music had staying power, music that would surely be around for a very long time. Musical preferences aside, Beatles music has staying power, as is evidenced by the resurgence of their music in the movie we saw that night, *Across the Universe.*

When we worked as teachers in Faith Academy, Andy was criticized by some in authority that he should not be teaching his students by referencing Beatles music. He was told not to wear his beloved Beatles tie to work because he was encouraging the kids to listen to *wordly* music. He obeyed the rules, but never agreed with them. He was privately quite upset that our teenagers were not expected to think for themselves and discern what music is harmful and what isn't. He also felt there were relevant messages in the music on peace and on love that could have come straight from Jesus. He didn't understand why having those words in a 'cool' rock and roll package made them unacceptable. He and I had some terrific early conversations on this. My spin on it was, as the English teacher, that this *wordly* music we were supposed to be afraid of was just poetry put to music. I was permitted to read poems in my classroom right across the hall that were from *wordly* poets' and perhaps even on topics that didn't have much to do with faith and God, so why didn't that extend to music listening? I understand that there were limits to what we should encourage our kids to listen to. I don't want them to get caught up in music that has bad messages either, but I think we could show them how to discern by insisting that the words do matter. I still say that to my own teenagers now: the words do matter. I know that they hear me, even if it is tough to enforce in this day of electronic music acquisition.

We also both agreed that music lyrics didn't have to get it right all of the time. There are lessons to be learned from the lyrics that get it wrong, too. There are characters in literature or in movies or on TV that we know aren't living right, we know them to have missed the messages our Bible teaches. That doesn't take away the value in those songs or movies. We both agreed that that could be beneficial, too.

To be honest, I was nervous when I was getting to know Andy's daughter. He and I had already fallen in love, so I knew that I loved her just because she was a part of Andy, but I didn't know if we'd *like* each other. Music is where we all could agree. Everyone knows that teenagers can be tough about their music, playing it too loudly and too often and at the wrong times, interrupting car rides and dinner hours and quiet evenings. Not so with Katie, though. She absolutely loved to play her music loudly, but she played *good* music. There were other adjustments to make, but with music as a common thread for all of us, we had a place to find agreement.

So, it makes perfect sense that the movie we saw together that weekend was a movie about music that Katie wanted us to see. It was a movie that used Beatles music to tell a story, a political story about the turmoil and trials of a country torn apart by human mistakes, drug addictions, violence and eventually war. In all of that, it is a love story about two young people who meet during this tumultuous time, right after the girl loses her boyfriend to the war in Vietnam. *Across the Universe*, is an expertly made film using Beatles songs performed by unknown artists to weave a culturally relevant love story. It was during that movie, as I sat next to Katie, that I had my first breakdown. Never in my life had I gone into such hysterics from either a movie or from a real-life event. Now, the two came crashing together.

The movie has a sad scene where a young girl is impatiently awaiting the return of her beloved from the armed forces as he served in Vietnam. She hopes they will be married when he gets back. Instead, two soldiers appear at the boy's front door and deliver the sad news to his weeping mother, carrying dog tags, a folded American flag, and a telegram. As the scene unfolds, a young man's voice begins an *a capella* version of "Let It Be." The scene changes, as the song continues and builds to a rainy funeral procession, black umbrellas, a hearse, a coffin and a burial scene where the girlfriend and the mom are holding hands in disbelief. I wept during that scene. Anyone would. If you've seen it, you probably did, too, but then the rest erupted.

I excused myself. I told Andy and Katie I needed to go to the ladies room and I walked out into the quiet lobby. No one was there. I had my cell phone in my hand. I did what I always did in times of true upset. I called Kerry on the west coast. Thankfully, she answered. I cried at her. I cried loudly. I sobbed like a baby. I was struck with a crippling sorrow. I had crumbled to the point of kneeling in front of these long, to-the-floor second story windows overlooking the town of Huntington on Long Island. I watched the evening traffic blur through my tears, watched the lights move into streaks before me. I couldn't get up. The idea that I would soon be planning a funeral was incomprehensible. *"Oh, my God. No, Lord! I can't do this! I can't do this! I can't! I can't go in there and laugh and talk with Andy and Katie and pretend like it's all okay! It's not okay! We can't just pretend that he's okay, that this is just another night out! We can't fake it! How long do we have?! How many nights will we have together?! Why are they just sitting in there like nothing is happening?! Something is happening! It's awful! It's terrible! It's real! The movie is sad. That funeral scene is really sad, but it's nothing compared to our reality! They were just acting. That dead boy walked off the set and went home to his family. Oh, Lord, do you hear me?! How can this be happening?! I cannot do this! I cannot. Why do you think I can handle this?! I cannot handle this!"*

And then I did handle it. I blew my nose, told Kerry I loved her and missed her. I thanked her for listening again. I wiped my eyes and walked back into the theatre, grateful we had chosen an activity that included a dark room to hide my tear-stained face. I sat in my seat as Katie whispered that I had missed the small appearance of Bono in the movie, the lead singer in *my* favorite band who sang a Beatles tune in a silly scene I saw on a later viewing. Then I knew that I had to fake it, too. Andy was doing the right thing. Why scare Katie now?

I'm reminded of another movie scene now. Remember in *Titanic,* when the families who had lower cabins realized they were not able to get to the upper decks, to the lifeboats? The moviemakers put together a beautiful scene where a Mom is pulling up the covers on her two peacefully sleeping children as the water level rises in her cabin. She is not frantic or crying. She is maintaining peace for her children in those last moments, realizing that the alternative would rob her children of their last moments of peace. There are no words spoken in that scene, and perhaps it's only a momentary flash on the big screen, but it is etched in my memory. It is a powerful notion, that as parents we will go to such great lengths to protect our children. I imagine that if I were that character, I might be running around frantically trying another plan, waking the kids and asking them to help. These parents chose better.

As I sat in the movie theatre next to a somewhat worried, but peaceful Katie, confident that her Dad and I had it under control, I learned this. We listened to the lyrics from the song, "Across the Universe." As the singer repeated the line about how he believed his world would never change, convinced nothing *could* ever change, it occurred to me that the ignorance Katie had was more precious to me than the knowledge I had. Why would I want her to feel the panic and the misery I was feeling? Why fixate on the truth of his dying? If we cried our way through these days, they would soon be gone. If we lost another moment, then shame on us. We couldn't waste time crying in the movie, or at the dinner table. We chose instead to laugh together that night, and on Thanksgiving and on Christmas and in every other moment God gave us. I think we chose well.

12

POSTCARD FROM THE D'ANGELO'S IN PHILLY

Date: November 9, 2007
Subject: Postcard from the D'Angelo's in Philly

Hi all,

Firstly, to all who have been praying with us and for us, thank you! We feel lifted and energized and supported. There's no other way that we could be facing this experience with such joy; it's the joy of the Lord that is our strength! Please continue to pray.

I am typing at a computer at the cancer center. We saw only one doctor today, but have a day filled with appointments for tomorrow. We spent this day mostly on paperwork and orientation. It is an amazing place. We feel very welcomed, supported, and optimistic here. The idea of whole-body wellness is in every aspect of the program, even on the shuttle buses and in the limo or car, we are given healthy food and drinks to keep us nourished. Kindness and love come from all. As New Yorkers, we're having a hard time finding there isn't a catch...and there isn't.

It was so unbelievable to go to their organic cafe -- not a 'cafeteria' -- for lunch and sit beside another man who was diagnosed with pancreatic cancer. He looked very healthy and hopeful. That man has already been under treatment for 25 days. He's been staying here. He lives in Massachusetts. He encouraged us that we had made a good decision in coming to Philly. Many others have been put in our path with similar testimonies.

Some of you already know that we did get a bit of good news on Tuesday morning. We saw a surgeon out of Stony Brook University Hospital's Cancer Center. He feels that he COULD operate on the tumor, but he did indicate the risks that that would entail where Andy's heart is concerned. We are seeing a surgical oncologist here tomorrow. His opinion will help us make a decision about whether it would be better to attempt to shrink the tumor first, then operate. ???

Thank you all for your love. Andy and I are so blessed by the support system that you all have created

for us. Thank you. Thank you. We'll write more when
we get home -- probably on Friday afternoon.

With much love,

~Catherine and Andy

ps. We are beginning to see God's divine plan in
all of this. Hope. Love. Joy. Peace. :)

13

TO PHILLY FOR FIVE WEEKS

Date: November 14, 2007
Subject: To Philly for 5 weeks

Hi again,

I've written and deleted this email three times already. I think I'm just exhausted. Forgive me for not getting it to you sooner. I also haven't been very good at answering my phone or the messages left on the machine. I am hearing your messages, though -- and I'm so grateful that you've left them. We are encouraged and lifted by your kindness, generosity and love. Through the generosity of friends and family, we are almost fully able to pay for Andy's stay in Philadelphia. The rate is very reduced by the center, but there are still some lodging costs while he's getting therapy as an out-patient. Thank you for helping us. Our peace and joy would be impossible without you. :)

Andy is leaving for Philadelphia tonight on a flight out of MacArthur Airport in Islip. He'll be there for five weeks undergoing daily radiation therapy and oral chemo treatments. I can't go with him yet. He'll be alone until I drive there on Friday afternoon. I'll stay for the weekend. I'm taking Andy's car. It's more reliable. (Judi and Esther: thanks for the driving lessons on the stick shift!) The kids will be with me. I have not yet returned to work. I'll make a second attempt tomorrow.

We really don't know how often I will be able to go to Philly or where the kids will be. We've been throwing around a lot of ideas; I could even take them out of school for a few weeks, homeschool them for a bit in Philly, and let them be a part of the healing. Perhaps it will be a better way to keep us all together. ??? We have to see what Andy's needs are as we go day by day. One day at a time...

When Moses was taking the Israelites through the desert, God sent them "fresh manna' every day. He gave them specific instructions not to gather and store it for the next day. When they didn't listen, the manna (food) would rot before the morning. They had to wait for God to bless them with the next day's nourishment. God has promised us the same. We are given 'fresh manna' every day. We are given JUST ENOUGH for today and no more. We can think of tomorrow, but we really can't plan for it. We are forced to trust God that we will get more of what we need with the new day. So, here we are.

We know that Andy's going to follow the planned treatment from the Cancer Treatment Center in Philadelphia. At the end of the first five weeks, they expect to do the surgery to remove the (shrunken) tumor. They refer to this surgery as the 'super bowl' of surgeries as it is quite involved. The tumor is, at this point, around and next to major blood vessels. They would need to be by-passed. This is, naturally, an increased cardiac risk for Andy. After the surgery, he will get another, more intense round, of radiation and chemotherapy. We may prefer to have the surgery on Long Island. ??? Again, one day at a time...

We are praying for the best: that the radiation shrinks the tumor so quickly that they decide to give him another round of radiation immediately following. If it is shrinking well they will opt NOT to do the surgery! This is not unheard of. In fact, it appears that his tumor began as a group of cysts. Apparently, that type of tumor responds very well to radiation. Couple that with Andy's determination, state of mind,

and prayer and we are bound to see the best result! :)
All things are possible!

Please continue to pray for us. We both feel as
though we have been lifted and carried through the
past days by the love that surrounds us from God and
from all of you. We feel prayed for. We feel your support. Please pray without ceasing. I desperately told
God yesterday that He must be wrong. I don't think
I'm as strong as He thinks I am. I immediately heard
that God wants me to know that **He is strong enough**.
I have to fully rely on His strength here....not my own.

Be well and God bless,

~Catherine and Andy D'Angelo

14

HOW ABOUT A LITTLE GOOD NEWS?

Date: November 29, 2007
Subject: How about a little good news?

Hi all,

I hope that all of you had a wonderful Thanksgiving with your families. We certainly did. It's great how much more we have come to cherish the relationships and time with people we love. It's all that really matters, isn't it?

We are back in Philadelphia again. Andy has had 9 of his 25 prescribed radiation therapy appointments. He did have a few bad days of nausea, one particularly hard day and a few difficult nights, but mostly, he has been well. He has been feeling energized and prepared to fight. He's in prayer and meditation periodically throughout each day. In fact, he's feeling called to begin a prayer/spiritual discussion group here at the center -- similar to our Monday Nights at home. There are many people here who are spiritual and faithful. They seem to need him to organize them. God always has something for us, huh? ....always a way that we can serve him and bless others with our gifts.

We got some good news today! Originally, the medical oncologist measured the tumor to be four and a half centimeters in size. They said it was difficult to operate on at that size, so they hoped that the radiation therapy would shrink it. The surgical oncologist said that even if it shrunk one millimeter it would make the surgery easier to perform. WELL!...God had other plans! Today the medical oncologist measured the tumor to be THREE and a half centimeters in size!! It shrunk an entire centimeter! That's about 25% smaller in just a week and a half!!! We are giving God all the glory! Thank you for your continued prayer!

When Andy set up the apartment here I brought in little plastic soldiers to decorate -- y'know? "little green army men"? I put them all over the apartment, some in the bathroom, in the refrigerator, on top of the tv, on the dresser. I posed them to fight one another. (the green vs the white) to symbolize the battle that Andy's body is in against the cancer. They are to remind him to keep attacking the tumor with all that he can. Today, when I came in, Andy had set them up a little differently! Some of the green soldiers were knocked down. The white (blood cells) had defeated some of the green (cancer cells). He's a crack-up! He's even having fun fighting cancer!

I'm sorry that I haven't been able to write a lot lately. I have missed keeping in contact with you. It's comforting to know that you are all there cheering us on and praying for us. I feel so blessed as this Christmas season approaches to feel so loved. Please know that we truly love you all, too. We are grateful for all of your support (spiritual, physical, nutritional!, and otherwise). It's so hard to admit the need and even more humbling to allow others to bless us. Thank you. That's all. Thank you.

I will be back in New York on Sunday afternoon. Andy will be here at least until December 20th. Keep in touch and God bless you.

~Catherine D'Angelo

15

HOW DO YOU STAY SO POSITIVE?

Subject: How do you stay so positive?
Date: December 7, 2007

Hi all,

I asked Andy in an overnight phone call how he stays so positive. He gave a long pause and then replied with, "I don't know. (another long pause....) "God has just carried me through it. I know that I am not alone." I find it very comforting to contemplate this answer. Isn't it true of any situation that seems hard to endure? We aren't stronger because the trial we are in is big, we are just taking life one day at a time. We are given grace for this day and no more, just like everyone else. Thank you, Lord, for this day.

We got some more good news yesterday! Originally, the medical oncologist measured the tumor through tapping and listening -- like finding a stud in a wall with a stethoscope -- at four and a half centimeters. Last Thursday, it only measured three and half centimeters. Yesterday, he reported that it has shrunk even further to the point of immeasurable through this method. He has to wait to have a ct scan to know the exact progress. Wow! The thief is on the run! :) I can't wait to see how the toy soldiers are set up now!

I'm leaving for Philadelphia in a few hours. Please call or email us. In answer to the most-asked question: yes, we are expecting Andy home for Christmas. He should be finished with his treatment on the 20th. If they need to keep him longer, we will stay until the holiday and then return afterward. We have no reason to believe that they will keep him. We'll keep you updated.

On another note, I saw the surgical oncologist at the Baldwin Center in Stony Brook yesterday. They said that though the biopsy done on my breast last month revealed only benign tissue, they feel that architectural changes point in the direction of cancerous cells. They are beginning to form in a stellar pattern. She said that only a biopsy of the removed section (one quarter of the breast) would be conclusive. She wants to remove the quadrant, biopsy it, and make decisions based on that result. I am scheduled to have breast surgery on the 7th of January. She said it would be best to wait until Andy was home.

Andy will be home for four weeks after this treatment cycle ends. His doctors said that the radiation would continue to work in his system for two to three weeks after the cycle ended. We don't know what they will suggest we do afterward. They had originally planed to surgically remove the tumor, but they also said that it may not be necessary if he's responding well to the radiation. Keep praying. :)

Thank you, thank you, thank you for all of your help and support. I wish we could express how helpful the quick emails, cards, and voicemails have been. You are our community, our support system, our family. We feel your love. Thank you. Thank you.

Peace and blessings,

~Catherine

16

YOU BETTER NOT POUT

Date: December 18, 2007
Subject: You better not pout

Hey,

I know you know the Christmas song, "Santa Clause Is Coming to Town" -- Bruce Springsteen's version is my favorite. I was driving along on one of my trips from Philly, singing as usual. I heard myself sing that I'd 'better not pout or cry' and naturally, I started to cry. I am such a dope! Anyway, afterwards, it hit me that, if this song about secular Christmas could be so effective in getting us to look at the bright side - "for 'goodness' sake," then I should be able to smile all the more. I've got hope, love, peace, grace, and many blessings. We have friends and family that show they care continually. We are blessed beyond measure. We better not pout! :)

Here's the news: I just returned from Philadelphia with the kids last night. Andy was home for the weekend. We brought him back for his last five days of treatment. He'll be finishing this round on Friday afternoon, and then he's coming home for Christmas.

Andy's having a CT scan done before Christmas to confirm the exact size of the tumor. We know that it has shrunken, but we can't know exactly how much without this test. The test will also show if the tumor has shrunken AWAY from the major blood vessels that it had been entangled with. We will also see how much of the pancreas and liver are affected by the tumor. Last month the tumor was interfering with the function of these organs. The results of this test will be made known to us after the team of doctors confer about it. They will tell us whether they recommend surgery or another boost of radiation and chemo. It looks like they may be leaning toward the booster round because he's tolerating the radiation so well. If that's the case, he will return on the 26th of December until January 9th. That remains to be seen. We will see the doctors on Friday before we leave, and send info when we can. Please pray.

Wanna go to Shelter Island tomorrow night? Shelter Island High School is holding a benefit for Andy called, "Everything Goes" on Wednesday night, the 19th. His students came up with the idea to charge admission to watch the teachers compete in events the students have created. The teachers are being really good sports about this! The kids sound like they're having fun doing this selfless act of giving. They have been encouraging Andy all along with quick phone calls, emails, and cards. Family and friends are welcome to attend. It begins at 6:30 -- after a game is finished in the gym. Call me for more details. I will not be able to attend. I will be with Andy at the cancer center for his appointments. My Mom will be here at our house in Manorville with the kids.

Katie's just successfully completed another semester at school! She is doing wonderfully well, is registered to attend for next semester (thanks to God's grace!) and will be home in a few days for about a month.

That's all the news for now. We will continue to keep you informed. We hope to have a great report for you on Friday! Keep us in prayer. Thank you for the notes, cards, emails, and messages of hope and support. They keep us going.

If we don't see you, have a very Merry Christmas. Be well. God Bless.

~Catherine D'Angelo

17

BLESSED BE THE NAME OF THE LORD...IN ALL THINGS GIVE PRAISE

Date: December 23, 2007
Subject: Blessed be the name of the Lord...in all things give praise and thanks

Merry Christmas, all!

I am writing to you from HOME! We are ALL here. Even Katie is home. Sigh...it feels good to be home for a bit. Thanks, Mom and Dad for ALL of your help while we were in Philly. I know it's a tough time of year to be feeling sick AND caring for grandchildren with pets and homework and visiting friends and mealtimes for two days. We love you very much and appreciate your sacrifices. The kids are blessed with extra time with two wonderful examples of adults. (Wanna watch them again tonight?....just kidding....)

Can you still praise God if you don't get what you asked for? Can you still smile and trust him?

Our news from the doctors in Philly wasn't what we had hoped for. We cried. We yelled. Actually, we even POUTED! :) ...but not anymore. In all things give praise.

This morning I'm realizing something new as I'm going over the Christmas gifts we have for the kids. I am wondering if my kids will be happy with the gifts they will open. I want them to be thankful. I want them to be happy. Imagine if I had to watch them cry and yell after I'd given them gifts? Even if I couldn't give them what they asked for ...like cell phones...because I don't think they need them, I don't think they should have them when they're so young, and I don't think they're responsible enough to take care of them. I know better. I am their Mom.

...and yet, we question God's fairness when we don't get the gift that we asked for in the package that we asked for it. Doesn't he know better? Do we have faith or don't we? God does know better. He sees the whole picture. He will give us the perfect gift at the perfect time. We really just need to trust Him and be thankful. In all things give thanks.

After the CT scan, the doctors conferred and decided that radiation would be best. Yes, that is what we had hoped for...in a way. We hoped that the doctors would tell us that the radiation was working so well that we should continue it for 8 more days to shrink the tumor instead of surgically removing it right now. They DID say that, but they also said that they feel surgery is no longer an option. They feel that the tumor cannot be removed. The radiation may have caused scar tissue to form around the vein that was running next to the tumor. They did not offer us the choice to take it out. Radiation may still shrink it. They recommended that he continue radiation with chemo in a more aggressive form for eight more treatments. He would be finished on the 9th of January.

The good news is: the tumor HAS shrunken 1.5 centimeters! The cancer has NOT spread! He's still feeling fairly well....some nausea, but he's still eating.... only lost five more pounds. The tumor has shrunken AWAY from and CLEAR of the artery that was next to it. The CT scan shows that the tumor is responding VERY well to the radiation. There's a change in color around the edges of the tumor indicating that the tumor is dying.

What will we do? We've contacted Sloan Kettering again. We're hoping to get in to see the recommended surgeon there before the radiation starts on the 26th... not an easy task with tomorrow being Christmas Eve. We want to hear from another surgeon. Otherwise, the radiation IS working to SHRINK the tumor and the doctors in Philly are saying that Andy will be able to live WITH the scar tissue and tumor in this area at this size. Andy would just like it to be gone. We liked having the option of surgery.

Please continue to pray for us. We are in awe of the amazing feeling that supportive loved ones around us has brought. We do feel loved and prayed for. Please continue.

Many, many thanks to the staff, administration, board, parents, and students of Shelter Island High School. We are SO grateful (and shocked!) at the amount of support raised for Andy's treatment. There's nothing more we can say; thank you.

Have a blessed Christmas.

Tell your family members that you love them.

Live in today.

We love you.

~Catherine and Andy D'Angelo

18

To tell this part of our story, I go back to our first big decision during Andy's illness. Andy and I had decided to send him to Philadelphia in search of the best route to wellness we might find. Philadelphia is a three-hour drive, unless there's traffic as you're headed through New York City. We weighed out the pros and the cons as best we could and made this drastic choice to have him live in Philly during his treatments at the Center.

The Cancer Treatment Center there was surely a place that could encourage healing, even if other places could not. We felt directed to go there, comfortable with their plan for his healing, and sad about how it took him from our home. Maybe it was best to give a man time alone, in his own 'desert experience,' so that he could make peace with his life possibly ending or how to keep that from happening just yet. The decision was hard to make because we would be apart, and Andy would have to live alone in Philly for 5 weeks or more. He was not at a point where he needed my care. He was able to sustain himself, even if tired, in the tiny apartment they set up for patients to use during their treatments. They provided three meals daily at the center in an organic cafe there. They provided shuttle service to the Center or even in to town if he needed. Most often, Andy had visitors though. I spent as much time as I could in Philadelphia, at least every weekend. His brother, his Dad, his Mom, his friends all took turns for the other days. He was alone sometimes, but always with the idea that a visitor was on their way.

As for me, when I wasn't in Philly, I was alone. It was terrifying to imagine this as practice for the future, if my future was being a widow. It *was* practice, though. I got used to sleeping alone again. I got used to opening, or not opening, the mail when it came. I got used to checking the messages for myself and cooking for just me and the kids. It was really difficult to fall asleep, and I hoped to do that while talking to Andy on the phone, but he usually fell asleep before me, or didn't want to use his cell phone for that long. So, I cried myself to sleep a lot.

One night, I was startled awake. Andy was in Philly. I was in a deep sleep, and suddenly felt as if someone were in the room with me. I opened my eyes to see the image of a woman kneeling in prayer with her head bowed and her hands clasped leaning at the edge of my side of the bed. There was no sound, no words, no light, just peaceful prayer. I knew in a moment that I was seeing Mary by my side, and that she was praying for me. She wasn't praying for Andy's healing. She was praying for me. I knew this.

It's not a long story. No great message came from the spiritual world. I was merely comforted by the idea that Mary, the woman chosen to carry our Messiah, was praying for me. She said nothing. She didn't even lift her head or look at me. She was absorbed in prayer. I don't know how often we are being prayed for, but it was glorious to feel the love of her prayer for me.

I didn't know what to do with that. As quickly as I had noticed she was there, she was gone. I didn't touch her or even try to, though she was right next to me. It happened so quickly that I immediately tried to talk myself out of it, too. I tried to reason that it was a dream or that I hadn't had enough sleep and had been imagining it. I wasn't afraid, though. I felt peaceful.

I tried to call Andy in Philly to share it with him. He was of course sleeping, but we had always had a deal: we could wake one another in the middle of the night, interrupt one another's sleep, so that we could talk, laugh, comfort one another, and eventually fall back to sleep together. Andy said it often. "You can wake me up any time you want." Yes, part of that was about intimacy, but more often, we wound up giggling and whispering on our pillows side by side.

On this night, I expected Andy to welcome my call, as if he were sleeping beside me and I had tapped on his shoulder. Instead, he didn't answer. I called his cell phone several times before the sound finally woke him up. He was groggy and tired and didn't want to talk. I thought if I could just stay on the phone with him for a few more minutes he would wake up enough to understand the story I was telling him. He would be excited with me that something so amazing had just happened. He'd ask me all the details. He'd pray with me, but no. He was cranky from being awakened. He wanted to go back to sleep. I suddenly felt silly to have awakened him, and I wondered how real the vision of Mary could have been.

I went to sleep, too.

So, who would I talk to about this vision? People at work didn't talk about the Bible or prayer. Public schools on Long Island don't have a lot of spiritual discussion in them unless it's in hushed tones. My friends from church? No. Their background was the same as mine and didn't afford us any wiggle room where

Mary and visions were concerned. My Mom? Her family? No. Again, Baptists who don't put much value in Mary. I could only go to my father. My Dad was raised Catholic. He knew about Mary. I went to him. I told him what happened.

When I told him the story, I was a little nervous. He was the first person I told besides Andy, and that hadn't gone as I had hoped. I called him on the phone from my kitchen. I blurted it out quickly as I stood at my counter concentrating on the pattern in the Formica. I didn't want him to laugh at me or make fun of me. I wanted him to bring insight, and I wanted him to believe me, even though I knew that it must sound untrue from the outside.

He did believe me. He was pleased to hear about it. I could hear him smiling through the phone. He was excited even. My Dad then told me that since he had first heard of Andy's illness he had been inspired to pray the Hail Mary. I hadn't heard my Dad talk as a Catholic much at all through my life. He had attended the Baptist Church with us when I was a girl. Yet, he was revealing to me that Mary was on his mind too. He didn't leave the Catholic Church, exactly, but he was not attending it either. Our conversation that day had greater meaning to my Dad, I suppose, than it had for me. He had already been called to pray with Mary in intercession for Andy's health. He was pleased to hear that Mary might be revealing herself to me as a holy part of the spiritual world, one that I had never known.

I still didn't know. I had heard the Hail Mary, read the story of the Angel Gabriel visiting Mary and Joseph, knew about the birth of Jesus in a manger in Bethlehem. Was there more?

I was stuck on the song "Let It Be," too. I had always liked the song. Who doesn't? It's a beautiful, honest Paul McCartney creation. I'd always known the simple tune, but hadn't really paid attention to the words until I saw that movie with Andy and Katie. Now, I seemed to hear it all over: in the car, shopping in the store, even in the waiting room at the doctor's office. The song became very important to me. I don't know if McCartney truly intended to turn such attention to Jesus' Mom with the song, but it had that affect on me. Coupled with her appearance in my bedroom, and my Dad's admission of praying Hail Mary's, it made sense to me that I was being urged to pay better attention to the one they call, Blessed Mother. I took it all as a sign that I must learn to let it be in all things. The rain is falling on a day I wanted to be outside; let it be. What choice do I have anyway? Fussing over it doesn't change it and only makes my day more difficult. Andy is feeling nauseous and knows he will throw up again, right after he has eagerly eaten the first full meal he'd been hungry for in days. Let it be. Let it happen. What choice do we have? Andy is dying and must leave me here alone with three children and a mortgage, without his love and support. Let it be. Slowly, I was learning. Let it be. There's nothing more. Let it be. Who better to teach me this lesson than Mary? She watched her son crucified. She must have been tortured to see her child hanging on a cross calling out to God in great pain and anguish, lonely and set apart and in need of comfort. What could she do? It was the will of God. She had to let it be.

19

QUICK UPDATE FROM THE D'ANGELO FAMILY

Date: 1/2/2008
Subject: Quick update from the D'Angelo Family

Hi all,

I really mean it...I'll be quick! :)

Since our news before Christmas from Philly, we are now unable to surgically remove the tumor. We have been trying to get an appointment with a recommended surgeon from Sloan Kettering in NYC for a second opinion. Today, after much waiting, we FINALLY got a call from them. We will be seeing a surgical oncologist who specializes in pancreatic cancer on Friday morning (1/4/08)

Many have been asking how Andy is feeling. He has had some bad days in the last two weeks -- worse at night. He's having trouble chewing food that stays down and agrees with him. Unfortunately, he also feels nauseous when he's eating. (...not easy for a good Italian who has been taught to eat in happiness, in stress, at parties, and in solitude...) We aren't sure if he's having trouble with the treatments or if he was exposed to a stomach virus at some point. They told us that ANY germs could cause more extreme symptoms after exposure to the radiation and chemo. We don't know yet. We take this day-by-day. Sometimes, he feels pretty good, too. :)

We are still in prayer. We are still hopeful.

God bless.

~Catherine

20

ALL YOU NEED IS LOVE

SubjectL: All You Need Is Love...John Lennon
Date: 1/5/2008

John Lennon ran with Jesus' message of love: love your friends, family, spouse, God, and even your enemies. We know this, but do we really KNOW it? Andy has had so much time lately to pray and meditate, and this is the message he's getting. (...either from Lennon or Christ...??) He tries to explain it to us and for a moment I get it, and then life rushes back in with laundry and appointments and work and I need reminding again. Nothing else really matters at all, does it? It's just about love.

Thank you, all of you, for surrounding us with love. We have felt loved all through this trial. We have never felt so loved. Thank you. We needed the continual reminder that God's love is this BIG. It's not just a flickering moment. It lasts. It goes beyond the moment. It's REALLY big. It can carry us through anything. :)

The news: we went to Sloan Kettering yesterday. The surgical oncologist believes that he CAN do the surgery (called the Whipple). That's good news! :) They are trying to schedule it for February 4th. They sent him back to Philly to finish the last four days of radiation and chemo. He'll be back on Thursday for good. They would like him to stop taking the chemo after that and to rest, eat, and to continue regular light exercise from home! They want him strong for this surgery-- which they warned us could take his life. They also said that, although the surgery does come with substantial risk, (especially for a heart patient) he must have the tumor out to survive longterm. The doctor feels that it would be inevitable that the cancer would spread to the brain, lungs, kidneys, liver within a few years without this surgery. Now is the time to have the tumor out to best ward that off.

The doctor also remarked on how healthy Andy appears to be. He has only lost a few pounds during treatment. He's still able to eat. Most patients are not this fortunate. He is also still going to the gym on most days. He has a very good attitude and is stubborn...ahem...I mean strong. :) He is ready to fight the cancer and go to battle with surgery. All of this works in his favor.

He did not for a moment consider skipping the surgery. He is fully ready to move forward. Please stand with us in prayer over the next month as we prepare him: body, mind, and spirit. Thank you, again, for your constant support and assistance.

We love you, too.

21

PRAY WITH US ON MONDAY NIGHT AT 7:30

Subject: Pray With Us on Monday Night at 7:30
Date: January 19, 2008

Have you heard this one before? Read on...

It was flooding in California. As the flood waters were rising, a man was on the stoop of his house and another man in a rowboat came by. The man in the rowboat told the man on the stoop to get in and he'd save him. The man on the stoop said, no. He had faith in God and would wait for God to save him. The flood waters kept rising and the man had to go to the second floor of his house. A man in a motor boat came by and told the man in the house to get in because he had come to rescue him. The man in the house said, no, thank you. He had perfect faith in God and would wait for God to save him. The flood waters kept rising. Pretty soon, they were up to the man's roof, and he got out on the roof. A helicopter then came by, lowered a rope, and the pilot shouted down to the man in the house to climb up the rope because the helicopter had come to rescue him. The man in the house wouldn't get in. He told the pilot that he had faith in God and would wait for God to rescue him. The flood waters kept rising, and the man in the house drowned. When he got to Heaven, he asked God where he went wrong. He told God that he had perfect faith, but God had let him drown.

"What more do you want from me?" asked God. "I sent you two boats and a helicopter."

I woke up thinking of this joke this morning. For weeks I've been having recurring flood dreams with all sorts of imagery we could interpret all day. It seems, overall, that I'm feeling overwhelmed at times, but the waters do recede into manageability. This old joke came to mind when Andy and I were talking about the surgery he's scheduled to have in two weeks.

We have been praying for a complete healing. We will continue to do so. We want the tumor to shrink away to nothing. We want the cancer out of his body. We want him to feel well again. We believe wholeheartedly that **all** healing comes from God. We know that we can ask God for healing. We know that He can heal Andy without any doctors or surgeries at all. We also know that sometimes there is suffering involved in our walk. We understand that our learning comes from that suffering sometimes. None of us would choose the hard lessons, but it's often those hard lessons that have a lasting impression and bring about real CHANGE in our lives. The path that we should be walking on is hard to see sometimes. When that path gets narrowed and our choices are limited, we tend to walk where we belong.

So, knowing that through suffering we can be changed and enlightened and blessed, we can believe that God may choose to heal Andy in a different way than we may choose. In other words, God's sending us two boats and a helicopter...in the form of surgery. Who are we to tell God HOW to work His miracles? He can save us any way he wants.:) In so doing, He will bless many others (medical staff, etc.) who will get to see the miracle up close!

Thank you, Lord, for carrying us this far. Thank you for this day. Thank you for helping us to find the blessings in the middle of trouble. Thank you for strengthening our faith. Thank you for always being present and accessible to us through prayer. Thank you for humor and levity and laughter and music and friendships and family. We know you will continue to carry us. In Jesus' name, amen.

The news: I had breast surgery at Stony Brook Hospital on Tuesday. I'm sorry that I haven't written until now; this is the first day I'm really AWAKE. I have a tough time with anesthesia. Besides the groggy feeling, all I can say is, "OW!" and "Thanks, Mom, for helping with the kids and the mountains of laundry that come with them." :) The surgeon said that it **DOES NOT LOOK LIKE CANCER**. They won't be sure until the biopsy comes back, though. The pathology report will be back on Thursday. I have an appointment on Thursday morning. I'll email you with the hallelujah report then. :)

Andy has his pre-surgical appointment at Sloan Kettering in NYC on Friday (the 25th). He will also meet with a cardiologist about the heart risks and what to do about them. They will also be doing another CT scan to see the exact size and placement of the tumor now. Lastly, we will meet with the surgeon (Dr. Peter Allen, no joke) to find out the details on the surgery, recovery time, the effects of the surgery longterm, etc. We will get a LOT of info on that day. I will email you afterwards. The tentative surgery day is February 4th, the day after Superbowl Sunday. We already know that this surgery comes with a great risk for any patient -- and more of a risk for a hearth patient. Any info we get will help us to be prepared.

With all the above in mind, we are asking for another commitment to prayer. We will be together on Monday night (January 21st) here at our house from 7:30pm. All are welcome to attend. If you cannot be here, please agree to pray with us from where you are. Please consider being here in person. Praying together makes a great difference. We feel encouraged. We strengthen one another. Specifically, we are asking God to guide us through decisions, to grant our family peace in a time of great stress and to strengthen and heal Andy's body right where he stands!! God is BIG!! All things are possible!! :)

We hope to see you on Monday. Be well and God bless you.

~Catherine

22

MY PARTNER

It was back when Andy had a heart attack that I first felt alone. I spent many hours truly mourning the loss of the partnership we'd had even before we knew he had cancer. Andy and I had always conferred on decisions, planned our lives together, worried together, learned together. We had agreed to raise our children together, and to build a home for them together, and to praise God together. It wasn't just a song. We really lived it. We wanted to stay together. We wanted to be partners. We did not want to be alone anymore. We were together because we already knew that we didn't like to live life alone. We already knew that sharing life and love and joy and family and the trials that come with all of that is better, much better, than being alone.

Partners. In Andy I had a partner. We helped one another. When he couldn't sleep, I listened to his worries and scratched his back. When I was troubled, he let me cry with him, he patted my back in that "there, there" kind of way. He was forever, "there, there-ing" me to sleep. We calmed each other. We listened. We loved.

We comforted each other with an affectionate caring touch. We did this so often and so instinctively that we gave little thought to our surroundings. In church, we held hands, passing the Bible and the notebook from one to another. On Monday Nights, Andy caressed my feet in his lap or I rubbed his arm. In the car, we always held hands, as one of us slept and the other drove. Our natural way was through affection. People noticed, too. It was common for us to hear from strangers that they were impressed by how much we loved each other. It showed. We were in love, completely devoted to each other. We could argue sometimes, and they could be doozies, but that passion translated to all areas of our lives and didn't keep us from our affectionate ways. Most nights, we fell asleep holding hands.

To realize that after I'd finally grown accustomed to the comfort of a partner I would now have to forget it all was devastating. I didn't want to draw on that old self-driven strength of my earlier days. My stomach hurt. My knees were weak. I had burning eyes that wanted to close in the peace of sleep. I needed to cry. I felt nauseous and sad and instantly unable. I didn't want to be the care-giver. I wanted to have my partner back. I wanted us to care for each other. Worst of all, in my hour of upset I could not go to Andy and talk with him. I could not hurt his pride by telling him I now saw him as unreliable. I couldn't hurt him that way. I had to feel partner-less and not share that with the one who had been my partner.

I was instantly on my own. I was instantly alone. I had to rely on myself again. I had to make decisions for me and for the kids and for our family and our household. I could not rely on Andy for these things anymore. He was supposed to get well. Following that heart attack, his doctors had said that he could find healing in rest and change in diet and continued medication and eventually light exercise as rehabilitation. I had no idea that this phase would never end. I didn't know then that I would never have my partner back. Or maybe part of me did know, and that's why I grieved it so much.

Being diagnosed with cancer on the heels of a heart attack only solidified all of those feelings.

My life felt upside down. The loneliness didn't feel as temporary anymore. It was surely going to last a long time. I kept getting up each day and going through the motions, meeting the demands of parenting and housekeeping and teaching. On top of that, I had a whole string of new tasks under the heading of wife that included caregiver, appointment maker, researcher, courier, and sleep aid. Andy was very needy, but also very prideful. He needed my help, but had trouble admitting that or allowing it, and sometimes had trouble showing gratitude.

We went along this way until our relationship was stretched even further. It was on the day I was scheduling my breast surgery that it all came to a head. I realized that I would need care and that I would have to find someone else to care for me. This was a serious surgery, one that I could not put off, one that had grave worries attached to it, and emotional components, too. Operating on a woman's breast is a very delicate matter. With it comes great worry. We want to be healthy and cancer-free, but we'd prefer to do that without disfigurement and without loss of feeling or loss of beauty. On top of all the emotions, it was presumed that I wouldn't be able to move my left arm at all and that I would need help carrying or lifting for a few days or more.

I never considered that we had any other choices, so I asked my Mom to come help me. Why not? My Mom loves me. There was nothing to discuss. But, I was wrong. Andy was hurt. He wanted to care for me himself. He hated that I didn't want to rely on him, that he realized I didn't think he was able. I knew it was hurting him, but I had to make sure I had adequate care, too. I didn't believe that Andy was able to care for me as I had had to care for him, even if it were only for a few days. Telling him so was difficult, but realistic. I knew without my Mom that the house would fall apart, the laundry would fall too far behind, the kids would feel neglected and that I would then have to work twice as hard the following week to get our house back in order.

The discussion that Andy and I had about this was over-the-top emotional. We were surely capable of a blowup argument now and then; we are two very passionate people who are used to speaking their minds, but this one really hurt us both. We cried a lot. We yelled a lot. We walked away and slept separately for hours that night. There was no way to repair the damage. It was permanent. I hurt his pride, and he felt disrespected as my partner and my husband. I felt neglected and unloved in his inability to admit he couldn't care for me. I wanted him to admit that it was best for *me* to have my Mom come. I was holding in the words that my partner was gone. Andy was a very smart man. I think he heard them loud and clear anyway.

To tell the outcome of this part of the story, my Mom did come and help us during and after my breast surgery, but Andy cared for me physically. He came in to the recovery room, sat by my side in my sleepiness, hand-fed me sips of water and food to help wake me up, cooked for me when we were home. It helped us all to have Andy able to give to me this one last time. He knew I needed him. It's good to feel needed. That's not the point I was after in telling this, though.

Once I recovered, our roles reverted back to where they had been before. It was right that they should, but again, I was back to feeling overwhelmed and overworked and under-appreciated and lonely. All of these feelings are common among spouses turned caregivers. The loneliness that comes with caring for someone instead of living *with* them is very difficult to manage. The loneliest part of it is that there is no one to complain to. Who could complain anyway? Who would admit to feeling used, under-appreciated and resentful? These are the natural feelings of someone who is used to being loved back and suddenly is giving and giving and giving to someone who is necessarily selfish.

I understood this. It hurt me, but I understood. Andy had to be selfish. I wanted him to be selfish. I wanted him to concentrate on healing. We both wanted him to get better. Selfishness brought that possibility closer to a reality. I thought so, anyway, and I was willing to try anything. The sacrifice of my partner was a temporary arrangement at first, only turning permanent for me in those last days when it became obvious that he would not get well.

I know I run the risk of sounding like the selfish one at this point. I think I might sound bratty and childish, but it isn't so. I truly did give with all my heart, of my time, my resources, all my energy, gave up sleeping just to watch Andy sleep and be sure that he was comfortable. It never crossed my mind at all to not give. I am not at all sorry that I did any of those things. I was called to give. Now I am so grateful that I was given the opportunity. Isn't that what we are taught to do? To give? To love? To do for one another? To accept the calling that God has for us? These are the ideals spelled out throughout our Bible and depicted through the stories of the lives of those within its pages: Moses, Joseph, David, and, yes, Mary.

23

THE HALLELUJAH REPORT

Subject: The Hallelujah Report
Date: January 22, 2008

How is this for a fast update?

My breast surgeon from Stony Brook called. The pathology report came back. There's no cancer! I still have a Thursday appointment to take off the bandages, but other than that, I won't see them again until next year at the routine yearly mammogram.

Thank you, Lord. sigh...

~Catherine

24

CATHERINE AND ANDY
D'ANGELO

Subject: Catherine and Andy D'Angelo
Date: January 27, 2008

Here's the news:

We went to Sloan Kettering in NYC on Friday. Andy was scheduled for a whole bunch of appointments. Here's how they went.

Well...sigh...first the surgeon said that the tumor is not definitely operable and not definitely inoperable either. He said that he will only know once he is in surgery. If he finds that the tumor cannot be removed, they will close him up. If it can be removed, he will do it; but he again warned us of the possibility of death during surgery or soon after, and then warned us again about how the cancer could still pop up in other organs -- even if the surgery itself is successful. He said that our meeting with the cardiologist would tell us more about how to proceed. As expected, Andy, knowing the risks, wants to head to surgery.

Sigh...the cardiologist took his time telling us that Andy is definitely a high risk patient. He believes that his risk of heart failure during surgery is substantial. He knows that without this surgery, the cancer will spread. The cardiologist still is not comfortable advising us that surgery would be a risk worth taking. He did not (yet) give the necessary cardiac clearance needed for surgery. After having met Andy, he plans to confer with his colleagues and with the surgeon, and they will have a decision by NEXT Friday.

The pre-surgical testing was postponed until that Friday, also. The surgery itself, if it is to happen, is now tentatively scheduled for Thursday, the 7th of February.

The reports themselves are discouraging without Christ. He is the only reason we can sustain such news. We did waiver a bit; we are still standing. ("... struck down, but not destroyed..." ---thanks, Pastor Mike!)

It's strange. It seems that through the direct facts and stats and percentages, these doctors are still taking the individual patient into consideration. The facts remain that Andy is only 50 years old, exercising three times each week, eating healthy, of a constant healthy weight, and possessing of a positive attitude. This all seems to be important to the doctors. The cardiologist, in particular, seemed to be watching Andy for a reaction to his medical opinion. In typical Andy fashion, he interrupted the doctor's slow, relaxed discussion to begin putting on his shirt then his coat, then he began to pace around the tiny exam room. Next (GET THIS!) Andy put his hand on the door and OPENED it! --all while the doctor was still sitting and willing to discuss this further! The doctor was smiling and laughing with me as we watched the patient take control of the meeting.

Afterwards, Andy said two things in response:

"Well, I was finished listening to what he had to say." and

"Well, I guess now he knows what kind of personality I have, huh?"

His attitude is terrific! :)

So, Andy will be home playing his guitar until next Friday (2/1/08) when we go back into NYC for a 'final answer' from Sloan Kettering. Stay tuned...

God bless you. We love you. Please keep praying.

~Catherine

ps. As always, we'll be praying or singing or hanging out at our house on Monday night at 7:30. Come over already. It's so cool to meet with God right in our living room! :) Call us. Maybe we can get Andy to play a little guitar for us...???

25

DOCTORS SCHMOCTORS

Subject: Doctors "Schmoctors"
Date: January 30, 2008

Wow! Last week, Andy was given a prophesy that he would have to keep strong in his faith in the face of bad medical reports. At the time, he almost wouldn't accept that the word was for him. His faith is so strong. His attitude and outlook are terrific. The woman persisted. She even wrote it down on a tiny slip of paper. He was to remain strong in the face of bad medical reports. He was to walk by faith, not by sight. Now we really see why he needs this message.

Yesterday, the surgeon from Sloan Kettering called again. After a more careful look at his scan, they see a spot on the liver. It appears to them that the cancer may have begun to spread. They canceled any discussion of or preparation for the surgery and are scheduling a biopsy instead. A biopsy would reveal if the spot is, in fact, cancer -- and if so, what type. If it is not cancer, the surgery option is still there. They have not yet given us a date for the biopsy procedure.

Andy, as usual, is ready for the fight. He is not shaken. He is researching and studying alternative treatments. Maybe the surgery was the wrong way to go anyway?? Maybe the biopsy would make matters worse??? He's investigating. Please pray for continued strength. Gotta run to work...

~Catherine

ps. There is a healing mass with intercessory prayer at the Shrine in Manorville today at 11:30am. Andy will be there. All are welcome to attend.

26

ANDY AND CATHERINE D'ANGELO IN PHILLY FOR A DAY

Subject: Andy and Catherine D'Angelo in Philly for a day
Date: February 18, 2008

It's been a while since I've contacted any of you. Our computer's with the GEEK SQUAD getting repaired. I'm emailing from Andy's address. Reply as usual; this will be back to normal in a few days. Many of you have been asking what's been going on with Andy. There hasn't been much news since our last report.

To recap, we have been home from Philadelphia together since the first week on January. Philly told Andy that they could not do surgery to remove the tumor. They sent him home to rest for one month in anticipation of further treatments in the month of February.

During that time, we were seeing doctors at Sloan Kettering in NYC to try to find another opinion on the surgery. As you know, while they were deliberating on whether Andy's heart was in a a condition that could sustain surgery, they found a spot on his liver on a CT scan. They presume that to be cancer as that is the place where pancreatic cancer is known to spread first. They were scheduling a biopsy that would necessitate Andy coming off some heart meds for five days (dangerous in the first 12 months after a heart attack) when we asked for some time to think it over. If the biopsy came back as a malignancy, they would not consider the surgery. If the biopsy were to come back benign, they would go back to the difficult decision about surgery.

Andy has instead tripled his efforts in the area of natural medicines. The idea is that we all have cancer cells in our bodies that we are usually strong enough to fight off daily. When our immune system is weakened by something (physical, emotional or environmental changes for example) our bodies provide conditions that allow cancer to grow. Andy is taking many supplements and has completely changed his way of eating to support his immune system. He is still fighting very hard against this cancer. We are also still considering Andy and all advice from the medical community. We are headed to Philly tonight for an appointment Tuesday morning. We would like to hear what they believe his options to be without surgery. Stay tuned...

On that note, be aware that we will not be here for MONDAY NIGHT. So, how about Tuesday instead? If we wind up staying longer in Philly, we'll email asap. We expect to be home Tuesday afternoon.

How's Andy feeling? He's having trouble sleeping and sometimes he's sick after eating, but he keeps eating every meal, and he keeps going to cardiac rehab and to prayer services and to family functions. He's driving to see friends and staying in touch through email and on the phone. He is happy and peaceful and rarely in pain. As is his nature, he's researching and reading a lot about alternative cancer treatments and wellness. He is playing his guitar NON-STOP. Our home sounds terrific. :) Many nights the kids and I fall asleep to the sounds of him playing.

So what are we doing for encouragement? Well, it's getting harder to stay strong, and anyone who knows me well knows that I'm having a very hard time. I cry when I'm distressed, so I'm not wearing a lot of eye makeup lately!:) That and prayer are the two best weapons I have for fighting off the blues. Music, family and friends are the other defenses. My faith is strong, but it's been shaken. If Satan can't use the weapons of fear, worry, and anxiety on Andy because he is so strong, he will go for the next best thing: the people close to him. I feel so under attack spiritually. It is a battle for me to stay joyful. Please keep us in prayer. We need strength as a family to weather this storm.

Thank you for everything. I will be in touch after our trip.

May God bless you all for your supportive friendship and love.

~Catherine

27

IT'S BEEN A LONG TIME

Subject: It's been a long time...
Date: March 5, 2008

Here we are!

I know its been a long time since I've been able to update you all on Andy. It's been hard to be out of touch.

sigh....here goes...Andy has not been feeling well. He has been sleeping a lot more, and he's having trouble eating. Our trip to Philly over the school vacation wasn't really helpful. They told us that he had lost ten pounds since his treatments ended at the beginning of January. (He's lost a bit more since then.) They recommended six months of chemo that we could get through Sloan's annex in Commack.

Our visit to Sloan was much the same. They also recommended chemotherapy, but a mixture of two types instead of just one. Andy hasn't yet decided if chemo is the best course of action.

Sloan also told us that the spot they saw on the liver is actually four different, oddly-shaped spots within the liver. We saw the CT scan. The spots are presumed to be the cancer spreading, but we wouldn't know that with certainty without a biopsy. He's not scheduling a biopsy.

Overall, I felt that neither place had given us Hope. They have emptied their bags of tricks. It is up to Faith and God's will and Andy's strength -- but then, it really always has been anyway, hasn't it?

The doctors here have noticed that he is beginning to jaundice again. They have scheduled an ERCP (don't ask me about the letters! It's some crazy string of medical terms that means they're replacing the stent they put in the common bile duct in November.) That should relieve the jaundice and the fatigue and the stomach upset. He should be able to eat normally again. We're both looking forward to that. Once his digestive issues are cleared up, he can go back to his natural foods to boost the immune system. He has been eating mostly Rice Crispies since last week. Doctors recommended just eating WHATEVER would stay down without distress, so the cancer-fighting diet has been suspended. The procedure is scheduled for tomorrow (Thursday 3/6/08) at Mather Hospital in Port Jeff.

I've gotta run, but I'll write again soon. Keep in touch, and be well.

~Catherine

28

EMERGENCY ROOM VISIT PROVES WELL WORTH IT

Subject: Emergency Room Visit Proves Well Worth It!
Date: March 16, 2008

Well, we've had a rough couple of weeks here. Andy has mostly been in bed, eating VERY little and in increasing pain. We were advised to go to the ER over this weekend if his pain persisted. Andy asked me to take him in last night.

Don't worry, though! This story ends well! After HOURS and HOURS at Mather's ER, we came away with a good report! The CT scan showed NO PROGRESSION of the cancer! In fact, there is reason to believe that it may have decreased in size and potency! The spots on the liver are appearing to be indistinct and the liver levels are only slightly elevated.

The tumor by the pancreas is reported to be "eroding" or dying away. There are no new findings of cancer in any other organs. (Say, "Hallelujah!" here!)

So, they sent us home at 4:30am with a new pain medication and more hope. He has been eating all day with no major difficulty! They said that this pain and discomfort were likely due to pancreatitis (painful inflammation of the pancreas that radiates to the entire abdomen and even the back) caused by the procedure ten days prior. Now that he's eating again, we plan to fight the cancer with nutrition and prayer. If Andy chooses to agree to chemotherapy treatments, they will begin on the Monday after Easter. He is still undecided on that.

THANK YOU ALL for the MANY prayers that went out for Andy on Friday. That was the hardest day for him with pain. He is now feeling relief.

...and we can still laugh! Try this one...

I wanted to clean our hands when I found out that there was a patient nearby in the ER who had a confirmed case of the flu. I was reading different containers of wipes aloud to Andy so that I wouldn't grab the harsh disinfectant wipes meant for cleaning equipment:

"Sani-cloth? ...What do you think the purpose of Sani-cloth is?"

Naturally, Andy replied, "He brings presents to children all over the world on Christmas Eve."

The sound of laughter filled the ER. I guess I should have seen that coming. Gotta love those IV pain meds!

"Thank you, Lord, for your continued comfort and strength. Thank you for Hope and mercy and peace in our family. Thank you for angels around us by night and by day. Thank you for joy and laughter! Amen."

Be well and God bless,

~Catherine

29

EASTER

A ndy has one sibling, a younger brother named Steven. He is a family man and works with their Dad as a self-employed painter in the family business. His passions include the Yankees, playing lotto in the hopes of winning it big, and then using his winnings to buy the car of his dreams, which varies depending on the year you ask him. Steven and Andy had a great relationship. They were friends and brothers. Andy played lotto with him, they watched the Yankees together (even if only through the phone) and went to the New Car Show held in NYC at the Jacob Javitz Center once a year on Easter weekend.

On Easter weekend of 2008, while Andy continued to battle cancer, but with greater difficulty, he remained determined not to miss the yearly ritual with his brother. I think Andy truly did know that he would not likely make it to next year's show. He would never again speculate about winning the lottery as he walked through the show gawking and dreaming about the cars with a hopeful, "After tonight...." Together they always joked that after their winnings came in with that evening's lotto announcement, they could afford to buy the car they wished for.

On this, Andy's last trip to NYC with his brother, I prayed for him. I was so worried that Andy would not be able to make it through the day. I worried that he'd be unable to eat anything or that he'd get sick and need a bathroom and be unable to find one. His digestive system was a mess. I worried all day long. He took our 12-year-old son Matthew with him to the show. This last day trip holds many memories for all of them.

I was lying on our bed in the peaceful calm that preceded the return of Andy and Matthew and the in- evitable rush to find a good dinner for all of us on this night before Easter. We still hadn't dyed our Easter eggs. I still hadn't ironed the tablecloth in prepara- tion for dinner. I still hadn't finished planning dinner. I still hadn't had the chance to sneak out and collect things for the kids' Easter baskets. I planned to leave the kids with Andy once we were all settled and run out to do that. I was resting for just one more moment before a busy night.

I heard Andy's car pull in the driveway. Then I heard the front door burst open and Andy's feet heavy on the staircase as he rushed up to me. He was breathing heavily when he appeared in the doorway, and he was doubled over at the waist. The grimace on his face showed me how much pain he was in. I'd never seen anyone in this much pain. He blurted out how his day went. He said he couldn't believe he was able to walk through the streets of New York or that he was able to drive at all to get home. He said the pain was unbearable.

Usually, if I just laid my hands on Andy's skin somewhere I could calm him, take away the panic that intensified pain. I immediately did this in an attempt to soothe him to sleep, let him rest from this very full, tiring day. He got onto the bed next to me. I tried my best to help. We waited. Nothing changed. Nothing helped. Nothing worked. He was still in intense pain. I could see that the pain scared him. When I suggested that we go to the emergency room, he eagerly agreed. I quickly arranged for my mom to come out to stay with the kids while I drove Andy the 45 minutes to the hospital.

The ride in the Explorer was extremely tense and unnerving. Andy was rocking back and forth in pain. He was holding his belly, then his back, then his head, then his chest, complaining of nausea, urging me to hurry or watch out for cars ahead and red lights. By the time we reached the parking lot, Andy was shouting that we couldn't even park the truck; we had to pull up at the door and abandon the vehicle so he would get quicker attention. I did that. I found a wheelchair for him and pushed him as quickly as possible to the doorway.

He got immediate attention from the excellent medical staff. They examined him and found that he was not in distress from his heart, but rather the pain was radiating through the many nerve endings surrounding the liver and pancreas. After about 30 minutes more of agonizing waiting through exams and medical histories, they gave Andy pain meds that helped the pain to subside to the point of bearable.

Andy dozed a bit as the hours passed into late-night and then into Easter morning. My worries mounted. My kids didn't have Easter baskets. They would wake up on Easter morning with no eggs hidden. They wouldn't have a normal Easter. Nothing about their holiday would be normal. Would either of us even go home tonight? This morning? In fact, nothing about their lives recently was normal. What kind of mother would allow her kids to feel so neglected. I have been so very focussed on Andy and illness and pain management and healthy eating and on the bills that mounted because of our loss of income. I didn't have the time

I usually had to devote to my children. They never came first lately. I then became frantic. I started to weep, then the weeping turned into crying, then the crying to hysterics. Now the overnight nursing staff was trying to soothe me. They told me to go home to my children, to sleep a bit if I could. They said they'd see Andy up to his room. He would be staying over for several days. They said that I could come back after I slept. I was confused and exhausted and upset, but I eventually agreed to do that. I made it home as the sun was coming up. I hid some eggs that my Mom and the kids had colored and stumbled to bed.

During this short hospital stay, we learned that the cancer was no longer isolated in Andy's pancreas and liver. Now it had spread to his lungs. They sent nurses and doctors to speak to me about Andy's eventual death and how I wanted to manage that: in hospice care at home or with more chemotherapy there at the hospital.

After some tears and lots of discussion, we decided that when the time came, we would call Hospice care and keep Andy at home. He was conversational, out of pain, hungry and eating. Andy was able to make this decision for himself. It was a good decision.

30

PLEASE SEND PHONE NUMBERS

Subject: Please Send Phone Numbers
Date: March 26, 2008

I was corrected recently when I said that I lost all of my phone numbers because my 'stupid phone' went KAPUT before I could transfer the numbers to a new phone. It's not the PHONE that was stupid... With that in mind, it would be great if you could send your phone numbers either to my phone or through email to this address. I haven't been able to contact everyone I needed to get to -- and this week has been a doozy.

Andy was admitted to Stony Brook Hospital on Saturday night through the ER. We spent our Easter there. He was in TREMENDOUS! pain. Doctors are in the process now of regulating pain medication so that he can go home comfortably. This is the opposite news from what we were given last week when Mather Hospital's ER looked at a CT scan, but Stony Brook's CT scan resulted in findings of progression in the liver cancer and spread to the lungs. They have recommended we contact hospice. Andy MAY opt to go for one intense round of chemotherapy first; we are still weighing that out.

He is comfortably sedated now on IV morphine. They are trying to switch him over to oral meds so he can come home without pain issues. He is eating, though in small portions. He is very sleepy. I'll let you know when he is home. That may be tonight??

We have always found that keeping strong in our faith was the most difficult just after a doctor appointment. They can really bring us down with stats and 'what if' scenarios. After five days of non-stop medical presence, we are finding that it's even harder. We have been reminded, though, that God is the only one who knows when we will be called home. We are foolish if we ever believe otherwise. WE are remaining hopeful. Who are we to question God? How silly that would be!!! He surely knows what is best for all of us. Trusting that brings great comfort.

Thank you, Lord, for your constant guidance, love, and comfort. Thank you for being trustworthy! We feel angels around us. We are in Your strong, capable hands. Thank you for your peace in our family. Holy is the Lord God Almighty. The earth is filled with His glory! In Jesus' name, amen.

Please continue to pray for healing in Andy's body. Our God is BIG!

Be well, and God bless you.

~Catherine

31

LET IT BE

Subject: Let It Be
Date: April 10, 2008

I haven't been able to write in a long while. I'm sorry about that...and so is my voicemail box! Both my answering machine and my cell phone have been full several times this week. I know that you all need to know how things are going. I would have liked to email sooner; it's been a crazy time.

Andy is now set up with hospice. We have been told that he is in the end stages of this disease. We are sad, but we can still count our blessings.

~Andy has had heart disease for years. We have all been prepared for that sudden phone call that says that he has had a heart attack and that we have lost him. Instead, God gave us this gift of being able to say goodbye to one another. There aren't any words that we have to take back. There aren't any words that we wished that we'd said. Count this as blessing #1.

~Many of you are aware that pancreatic cancer is a HORRIBLE way to die. Unfortunately, I have read a lot about it myself and do know that there is a mass of nerve endings located behind the pancreas. The pain that is often associated with this cancer is not able to be controlled by medication. Eventually, many patients are sedated because pain meds are no longer effective....not so with Andy. He did have a bout with pain just before he entered the hospital that was easily controlled by pain meds there. Since he has come home, we have slowly decreased his medication to about one-third what he needed at the hospital. He is STILL NOT in pain. He wants to reduce it further. No pain. Blessing #2.

~The symptoms that he does have are that he can no longer eat at all, and he is vomiting often even without eating. At first, this sounds terrible, too, but understand that he is NOT NAUSEOUS. He has a sudden urge to be sick, and he is. Afterward, he is tired. This is presumably caused by the tumor's growth and the cancer spreading through the digestive system. No nausea is blessing #3.

~Dehydration is a very humane way to pass on into death. As hard as it is for all of us to consider that Andy will leave us now, it is best that we know that the course of dehydration is a blessing, too. He will fall asleep more often and for longer periods. This, too, is a blessing.

Andy has gotten MANY, MANY cards and emails and visits and gifts from people in his life that he has touched -- mainly students. This has done a world of good for him. As one looks at the end of their life, it is only natural to contemplate whether our time has been well-used. Andy, who has always been hard on himself, has always been one to think of a way to improve -- be a better husband, father, teacher, friend, colleague. He remarked to me that he thought he had more work to do on this earth. I guess he thought he hadn't made enough of a mark on us. To those of you who have already told him otherwise, thank you for helping me show him that he has. We would love to keep him longer, but he has touched our lives already -- even if we've only known him a short while.

So my last request to all of you is that you please take a minute to use the time that God has granted us to let Andy know that he has lived a life that has been worthwhile and useful and loving and...well, you know...

I will read all letters, cards, and emails to him. He will hear what you have thought to write.

As always, please pass this email to all who may be interested in knowing this info. I would love to say that you may all come and visit, but unfortunately, he's truly not up to it. Call and check. You never know.

Lastly, I had a great moment of lucidity with Andy yesterday that just blew me away. I wanted to tell him how I truly felt USED by God in our current situation. I know that I'm supposed to be honored by 'being used by God' but I was feeling really upset about it instead -- like a cheap date kind of thing. I felt that God had just set me up here, to help Andy through a tough time... and he USED me to do that. He let me fall in love with someone who is perfect for me. He let me feel compassionate and nurturing through his illness. I felt like God left me with only a broken heart.

Immediately, upon hearing this, Andy said, "Imagine how Mary felt," and I did.

Imagine how she must have been broken-hearted and felt used to be given a perfect child to nurture and love and then watch suffer and die???? She knows how I feel. I guess I'm in good company. :) ...and I'm not mad at God about it. In fact, if he'd asked me about it first, I would've said yes. The benefits have far outweighed the heartache.

Be well. Love your family. Enjoy every moment. Cry when you're sad. I love you. Thanks for everything.

~Catherine

ps. Andy's Mom Livy arrived yesterday and actually said that her flight was fine! She had no turbulence and actually had a stranger hold her hand the whole way! They became great friends. She will be contacting her to fly home together, too. *Thanks, Lord!* :)

32

ITALIAN EATING

Andy's parents were both there when he died. They stayed by his bedside in his last days in complete disbelief. Their bodies and faces showed signs of wear. They were tired and confused and distraught. Being second-generation Italian immigrants, they were both drawn to feeding Andy as part of nurturing him. Italians eat for more than just nourishment. I am a skinny German girl who used to protest what was put before her at the dinner table as a nightly ritual when I was younger. It took me a while to understand that Italians behave differently.

Socially, I had never been comfortable eating in front of others. I never wanted to "eat over" my friends' houses. I didn't want to reject their food with my queazy stomach or my turned-up nose. I liked peanut butter and jelly, and I liked Frosted Flakes. Other than that, I was rough to feed. I looked undernourished as a kid, and honestly, far too long into my adult years as well.

Naturally, one hundred percent-Italian Andy wanted to eat every time we got together. He took me to dinner, cooked for me, talked about food. Likewise, his parents wanted to meet me over meals. They prepared elaborate dinners, they planned evenings out in high-priced, full-service Italian restaurants. They drank fine red wine with dinner. And, the conversation over these mealtime gatherings was about travel or parties or family memories, but somehow, always had its foundation in food. "Where did you eat when you went to Italy?" "What kind of food did she serve when you went to the Christening?" "Remember when Aunt Sofie used to yell on the porch for us to come in for lunch?" Food was used in times of celebration, in times of mourning, in times of loneliness, in all things social. They taught me that Italians eat, not just for nourishment, but as part of living. Eating is exciting and varied and a wonderful experience when you grow up in an Italian family, very different from what I ever experienced.

So, when Andy's cancer grew in his digestive system, it was far too much for his family to understand. Add to the above list that when Italians are sick or sad they also eat. Unfortunately, Andy could *not eat*. It troubled him, too. He felt nauseous, but kept trying to change foods. He didn't consider stopping eating to feel less nauseous. He just acted as if he were looking for the right food to go down and stay down. Along with that came guilt. He felt like a failure when again he'd throw up. He felt like he had just chosen the wrong thing. He tried again, avoiding whatever it had been that kept him from being successful.

Likewise, his parents, who were staying with us most of the time in his very last days, acted as though they felt this way, too. I could relate to that in a very basic human way. As a Mom of two school-age children, I feel it is my responsibility to nourish them. If they get a stomach ache, or it they don't feel well, I more carefully manage what they are taking in at meals. We all understand this. We eat lighter in times of stomach upset. We lay off snacking and desserts if we are gaining. We do those same things for our kids. Understanding that made it that much more difficult to watch Andy's parents make continued attempts to make him well.

His Dad kept asking Andy if he was hungry, even in those last days when he was only awake for a few hours. As soon as his eyes would be open, his Dad would rush to him and try to feed him as if he believed that it was the only way he could help. It was beautiful to see him holding on to a belief held for generations passed that good food was the key to everything. It was very sad to see him tormented by the way this time-tested method couldn't serve them in the face of pancreatic cancer.

Andy's father fed him his last meal. I'd love to report that it was some great pasta dish or that he had had a taste of an amazing pot of sauce, but it was Chinese take-out. We had all been ordering our dinner in anticipation of a long night awake with Andy on little energy. A friend of ours offered to have Chinese take-out delivered to the house. As we were deciding what we should order, Andy woke up from his sleep to shout out, "I'll have lo mein!" I laughed. I thought this was silly. He hadn't had solid food in more than a week. He was drinking sports drinks and ginger ale and cola and even chocolate milk, but hadn't been eating solid foods. His Dad very eagerly responded to that call, though. He ordered the lo mein, repeating often that Andy had asked for it. He was truly beaming. Could he really believe that eating Chinese food would make Andy well? I don't know, but I know he felt that even the request was a step in the right direction.

Andy ate one or two hearty bites of lo mein fed to him by an incredibly worried and loving father. The scene was reminiscent of a young Dad with his six-month-old. The expression on his face was full of tenderness and concern and hope for a future. He hadn't yet accepted that his son was dying. Several hours later, Andy took his last breaths, his Dad still in disbelief.

I wasn't prepared either. I guess I just expected to know first. I thought I would get some word of knowledge from the Holy Spirit to prepare me for the moment of Andy's death. Looking back, I realize how obvious it must have been, but I didn't know at the moment.

On the day before Andy died, I had an appointment for a therapy session. I almost didn't go. I felt that I was truly needed at home, that I wanted to be with Andy every second. I also knew that I needed to get back in touch with our psychologist. I knew that big changes were on the horizon, and I did not know how to manage them at all. I had never lost anyone that was very close to me. I had never cared for someone until they died. I had never touched a dead body before. The fear of going through all of that without support won out, and I drove the 45 minutes to the appointment.

On the drive home, I got a phone call from the hospice nurse. They were visiting once each day. They gave me information, answered questions, helped me care for Andy. I reported to them how the night before had gone, what I was planning for the coming day, etc. I had been expecting them in the afternoon, but, as it happened, they came early. I missed the appointment, so the nurse gave me the courtesy of this phone call.

I was driving over the speed limit, trying to get home as quickly as I could. I wanted to talk with her face to face. There were family members who were trying to make decisions for Andy that were not in alignment with his wishes. Emotions of all were at a height. Anxiety, confusion, and upset were easy to find. We struggled to feel peaceful.

While still in the car, the nurse consulted with me through the phone about what she had seen in other deaths from cancer. She said that at this point, she expected Andy to get sleepier and sleepier. She thought that he would not be getting out of bed to use the toilet soon. She wanted to prepare me for how to manage that and keep his bed clean. She told me that I was doing well for him with his medications, correctly stopping his heart and blood pressure meds and maintaining his anti-anxiety meds, but not raising the levels. She assured me that I was doing a great job caring for Andy. She told me that his sleepiness would likely increase to the point of only occasional waking. Then, he would pass. She told me that this could take as long as two months.

Every bit of information that she fed me through the phone was processed through this filter of emotion and upset. Her words were important to remember, but they punched me in the stomach, too. I kept feeling waves of the reality that Andy was really dying, that we had agreed to stop his treatments and that we had agreed that he get the opportunity to die at home under my care. I tried to keep driving quickly through tear-streaked vision. I made it home in time to greet the nurse on the front porch.

The sun was shining warmly. The birds were singing happily. It seemed odd even then. I smiled and welcomed the nurse to our home. I invited her to sit with me for a moment. After just a few minutes of talking while I fought back a huge lump in my throat and an endless well of tears, I told her I was tired. I told her how Andy kept trying to get up in the middle of the night and that I hadn't slept. She saw my exhaustion and told me that she thought I was small enough to crawl in beside Andy in his hospital bed. She said that many couples did that. They just slept together in those last hours because it provided comfort and rest for both people.

I couldn't say goodbye to her fast enough. I wanted to run up the stairs to Andy. The nurse quickly left, and I did run up the stairs. I was in hysterics by the time I had turned the corner into my bedroom. Andy bolted up to a sitting position and yelled, "What?

What is it? What's the matter?!", as if he still didn't understand that he was dying and his death would make me cry.

I ran to his bedside and made my apologies to his mom. She had been staying by Andy's bed as he slept while I was out. She let the nurse in, put on coffee, straightened the clutter. I told her I needed to be alone with Andy. She obediently closed the door in full understanding. I kept telling her I was sorry. I couldn't imagine someone asking me to leave the room if one of my children were in this condition, but I had to. She told me again and again that it was okay.

Andy touched my face, smoothed my hair, and kept asking "What?" as he searched my eyes. There was love and sorrow and pain on his face. There was also a bit of confusion. He had been awakened from a deep sleep when I burst into the room. I told him I didn't want him to leave me. I told him I was sad. This was all too sad. I told him to move over in that little hospital bed and I held his hand and fell asleep crying next to him. I didn't want that moment to end. Sleep was the answer for us both. The nurse was right. It brought us comfort.

Our dear friend Deborah, one of our Monday Nighters, knocked on the door a while later. I don't know how long we'd been sleeping, but she said she wanted to pray with Andy. When I rolled over to look at her, I saw reflected in her expression the scene that she'd inadvertently come upon: the helpless cries of a young wife, confused and scared at what was the inevitable, clinging to a love that was crumbling to bits in her hands. She whispered that she'd only stay a moment. She said that God had not told her to stop praying for healing, so she would not give up.

She came around to Andy's side of the bed. She put her hands on his arm and on his forehead and prayed and prayed. She wept as she prayed. She left, then. I stayed next to Andy until some task got me out of his bed. It would be the last time I would lay down with him peacefully.

There were visitors all night. There were visitors bright and early in the morning. We were never alone again.

On the next morning, I washed him, brushed his teeth, chose a clean t-shirt for him, even though it was much too big for him to wear now. I changed his sheets, placed the hand-made quilt at the foot of his bed. We kept going that morning, talking with Katie and with his Mom, totally unaware that we would never do this again.

Andy's death that night was as peaceful and even as joyful as it would be if it had been a birth. It was remarkable to me how similar the two experiences are. We kept soft classical guitar music on, we read Psalms aloud from the Holy Bible. We prayed out loud in the circle that was his closest family: his father and mother, his brother, his best friend, his daughter and me. We touched him and tried to meet all of his needs as his breathing changed and became labored, as his heart raced, as his temperature went up and his blood pressure went down. I held one hand in his and one hand on his pulse for the last moments of his life. We all talked to him through his last breaths, praying, saying, "I love you" one last time. It was very sad, but it was more beautiful.

It was after his pulse had stopped, while I still had my hand on the warmth that remained on his neck that I noticed the t-shirt that I had chosen for Andy to wear that morning. I pointed it out to his best friend, Tony, as he sat across from me. The shirt was black and had the cover of a Beatles album on the front. So what? Andy had a lot of Beatles t-shirts. This shirt said LET IT BE.

I knew there was no more that I could do. There were no other appointments or medicines or wellness plans to investigate. Letting God's will be done isn't necessary. His will prevails regardless of our letting it. It is only a lesson for us to learn to let it be.

It is in that last email of Andy's life that I explain to our friends and family about how important Mary is. When Andy asked me to *imagine how Mary felt*, I really did. It stopped me in my tracks. While talking with Andy that day, I was just building up steam to start complaining to Andy about God's choices for my life. I was trying to say that the Creator hadn't made good choices for me. Ridiculous! When Andy compared my complaints and true suffering over the past months to those of Mary, I was instantly humbled.

Imagine how Mary felt? What if we found ways in each day to imagine it? What if we tried each day to understand that God loved us enough to use us, that he trusted us to use us to help others?

What if we imagined Mary declining to serve God? Can we even imagine that? How would Mary have felt if she'd turned God down, like we have all done before? We see someone on the side of the road, perhaps, and we feel a tugging on our hearts to pull over and help them with their car or give them a ride, but we don't obey. We drive off because it's inconvenient to stop. God has to use someone else to be their angel, then, but not Mary. She understood that saying yes to God's calling would humiliate her and use her and leave her sad. That would certainly be inconvenient, but she was blessed more than she could ever have imagined, too. Caring for the Son of God in her womb, in her arms, in her life changed the world. Where would we be without Mary's obedience and the grace that her baby's life brings us?

Let's not forget the trust and love that God has shown for Mary in his choosing her to raise his son. That's powerful, too. Surely Mary was honored to be chosen and used by God. *Imagine how Mary felt.*

In my experience, the honor to serve changes the whining about the inconvenience, but it can be an effort to get to that. I do have to remind myself to *imagine how Mary felt* often. Otherwise, I can get bitter about giving. I can feel upset by people needing me and God using me as His servant. I can find it all too inconvenient.

Meditating on Mary's feelings brings me peace and eventual acceptance of God working in my life. When I can truly accept the road that I am on as the path God has chosen for us to walk together, I can then just let it be.

33

ANDREW D'ANGELO 1957-2008

Andrew D'Angelo

April 21st, 1957 ~ April 16, 2008

Our beloved Andy had a beautiful passing into the hands of

Jesus in the presence of his parents, his wife and children.

He did not have any pain.

His breathing labored briefly, and he passed.

God is merciful and answered many prayers.

We would like to ask that the family not be contacted at all tomorrow as we are planning a day of private rest.

Arrangements have not yet been finalized,

but are expected to be set for

Friday, April 18th

at Sinnickson's Funeral Home in Center Moriches.

Please call them directly to confirm times, get directions, etc.

Sinnickson's Funeral Home
203 Main Street

34

HOME

Andy got to know my friends from grammar school quite well after we were married. One couple in particular was Terry and Melissa. The four of us went out together to restaurants or to shows. We had long talks over bottles of wine, too. Those talks often turned to my past. They loved to share little bits of who I used to be with Andy, to give him a clear picture of how much he had changed my life, to provide the proof about how much of a blessing Andy really was to me. They gave validity to my complaints I'd shared with Andy about my past, of not being joyful and not being fulfilled, not being listened to, not being myself. It was embarrassing at times to have my close friends share intimate details of my teen years with Andy. He didn't know that girl to be Catherine, that insecure, too-skinny, awkward girl Terry and Melissa knew. He knew a much more confident English teacher, that was learning to eat like an Italian, even if I did still cut my spaghetti.

On one of Andy's Sunday night trips back to the Treatment Center in Philly from Long Island, Terry volunteered to drive. I was relieved to stay home with the kids, and Terry loves to act on impulse, so a spontaneous overnight to Philadelphia with his friend was a no-brainer. I assumed they would be talking for the ride and for the evening. Terry and Andy went out to eat together, and drove around to music stores as Andy contemplated which guitar he might buy. What I didn't expect was that they really got down to the nitty-gritty. Andy wanted to know if he had really changed my life for the better. I always said that he had. Other friends had always said that he had, but he wanted the details. Terry gave them.

A few days later, when I had come in to see Andy, he had this knowing smirk on his face. His expression told me that he was feeling vindicated and victorious. He finally revealed over dinner that night that Terry told him about how very much Andy had helped me to be the confident person that I had become, the kind of person who would be able to boldly write emails about my faith during times of trial. I was embarrassed to admit to Andy that I hadn't been something he would admire before then. I used to be someone who wouldn't have attracted him. I was very,

very fearful, anxiety-ridden and easily upset. I allowed people to be unkind to me. I used to be someone I didn't even like. I didn't like Andy knowing that I had been so different.

It turns out that it was right for Andy to get a true picture of who I used to be, to feel victorious about being such an incredible encourager that he lifted me out of that. He needed to know that he had made a difference in my life. Terry helped him to see that he had changed my entire family, starting with me.

In my discomfort, I made an effort to recover some of my dignity. Hiding behind a messy Monte Cristo sandwich with raspberry jelly, I asked Andy if I'd made a difference in his life. I really felt awkward asking him. I was so afraid that he would joke about it and never answer me. I was afraid that he wouldn't see a difference. I was afraid that he would say that I hadn't made a difference.

His answer was a surprise to me. He said that I had changed him spiritually. He said that he was always extremely private about his spiritual life, that he had learned through me to be bold. He said that through me his faith had grown. Even a messy sandwich couldn't hide my beaming through watery eyes. I now understood his expression when I'd first gotten there. He was proud to have made a difference.

We got back to our dinner for a while, talked about the kids, the treatments, the doctors, our jobs, our bills. Exhaustedly, we got up with our doggie bags and settled in for the short ride back to his temporary apartment there in Philly. Once there, he grabbed his old guitar and showed me how much he had been practicing. I laid down on the couch and looked around his apartment. I'd been trying to make this place of healing as much like a home as I could. I had been cleaning the floors and bathroom and putting his get-well cards around the room. I bought a few little things for him to hang on the walls. I noticed that he had been putting up posters and words of encouragement too. It was odd. I wanted him to feel at home there, but not really. I wanted him to miss our real home, too. I was sharing this with Andy when he revealed another truth about how I'd changed his life. He told me that, for the first time since he was a boy, he had a home.

Andy's parents were divorced when he was a young teenager. He was displaced, left to live with his best friend's family so that he could graduate with his class. He chose to do so because he didn't like how the place where his mom and brother lived just didn't feel like home anymore. He said that, since then, he'd been trying to find a place to call home. He shared that I had done the same for Katie. Each of them had a home at 20 Fairway Drive where we lived. They had a home together. Our family had a home together.

What images are conjured up in our minds when we consider the word *home*? Right away I think of where I am living now: the yard, my bedroom, my family, the pets. I feel the comfort of my home, I imagine the fire crackling in the living room, I smell good food in the kitchen. More realistically, I should imagine a pile of dirty laundry and a puddle from my puppy on the linoleum, but thankfully, in my mind's eye, none of those unpleasantries show up.

Regardless, it feels good to think of home. At the end of a long day, I want to be home. Even after a great vacation or some time away spent well, I long to be home. I like to be home. I like being home more than I like to be anywhere else. I think Andy had learned to feel that way, too.

When I truly need comfort, I instinctively run to my parents' house, instead though. I know I have my own home, and I'm an adult, but there are times that I like to forget that. I like to run to my parents' house. That is really my home. I lived there from age 5 to 23 when I moved out. 228 Mt. Vernon Avenue. That is where I learned life's lessons. That is where I lived when my grandparents passed away, where I hurt my foot on the front door and needed 6 stitches, where my friends slept over. That kitchen window is where we sat and watched the hurricanes pass and snow pile up outside. We watched baby birds being born in the birdhouse on the deck, and we had graduation and wedding celebrations there, too. The memories in the walls made that house our home. The moments we shared there just watching episodes of the Waltons or Saturday morning cartoons with our blankets and pillows in front of the big cabinet TV gave the place significance. It's not just a house to us, it's a home. If I need comfort, I know that just walking in and smelling our old house brings comfort. I plop on the couch and fall into easy, relaxed sleep. That's home. That's the place I want to be. I guess that was the feeling Andy had been lacking.

Doesn't everyone need that? Don't we all need a place where we lay our heads? Where our stuff belongs? Where we know every inch of the floor? A place where we get so used to mowing the lawn that we recognize the little dips in the property like no one else could? We know which doors stick and what trick to use to close the drawer in the cabinet on the left. We own it all, even if the mortgage papers still say the greater portion of the value is in the name of the bank. We feel like we own it. I feel like I own my parents' house too, even though my name has never appeared on their deed at all. It is mine in a way that doesn't make financial sense. It's just my place. It's my home.

It's like I have two homes: the one I created for myself, where I chose the carpeting and arranged the furniture, the one where I am making new memories for my own children; the one where I am responsible for maintaining and paying the bills and for cleaning up all the messes. Then there's the home where I retreat when I want to be cared for, when I am in search of comfort that doesn't include responsibility for the electric bill: it's my father's house. I love both places. In both places I feel comfortable, and I have a home. In both places I can relax, but with a different feeling.

Andy reminded me of the importance of *home* with his explanation of what it was like to live without it. He valued the home we had created together because he had missed it for so long. He loved being able to create a space like that for his daughter so that she wouldn't be lacking that feeling. He remembered the comfort of a cozy, safe home. He knew he had found it once again.

Where is Andy now? Has he been displaced again? Is he lost? Homeless? I don't think so. He is with his Father, in another home, one where he doesn't have to pay the mortgage or worry about the chores. Our Father has created a home for him.

How did he decide which home was better? From this side of Heaven, I can understand his longing to stay with us, to watch Katie grow up, walk her down the aisle, have a family, and to stay with me and be my partner and hold my hand as we fall asleep. At the same time, how could he resist the longing to be in the presence of the Lord? How could he want to be back here on earth when he is given a glimpse of being with his Creator?

There was a moment where Katie and I watched Andy have to make that decision. I know that death is in God' hands, but we watched how Andy was given the opportunity to use his own will to ask death to wait a few minutes, hours, maybe even days. He was given the chance to allow death to happen or to fight it off and spend more time with us here. This is what happened.

Andy did eat that lo mein fed to him by his Dad that night, but it didn't stay down exactly. Eating did not serve the function it was meant to serve. The food went down his throat, but somehow never became a part of him. Cancer now filled his body so very much that organs were no longer working. Who knows where that lo mein ended up in the cancer-filled organs he now had, but he soon felt quite nauseous and gave me the sign that he needed to be sick. I sat him up with great effort, allowed him to lean on me as I sat beside him on the bed with one arm around him and one arm holding a basin under his mouth. He wretched forward and then passed out. His whole body went limp in my arms. I shouted to his Dad to help me, to keep him from falling off the edge of the bed. We quickly realized that the best course of action would be to let him lay down again. So, even without getting his head back on the pillow, we leaned him back, his legs still dangling over the side. As we did this, I looked into his face. His expression was fearful and confused at once. His eyes were rolling back, then coming back into focus with mine. Without looking away, I shouted out for Katie to come in, for his Mom to come in. Andy was dying. I wanted us all to be there. I didn't cry. I didn't panic. I spoke in soothing tones. I held his head in my hands as I leaned over him.

His Mom, his brother, his Dad and I were all there. We just needed Katie to come in, then he could go. He could just peacefully die. Finally, Katie came in. She saw him and spoke up to him loudly, "Hey, Dad! What's your favorite holiday?" She was trying to wake him up. She was trying to get him to talk, to be revived. There was a brief moment where she waited and repeated herself, but then he actually answered her. His face lit up; he woke up. We all smiled and breathed a sigh of relief. A false alarm. We sat him back up in the bed and called the hospice nurse to have him checked. We laughed about how beautiful it was that just the sound of Katie's voice could bring Andy around. It was more testimony to how much he loved her.

Unfortunately, that's not how Katie took it. After the nurse came by and had announced that by his vitals he had less than 24 hours left to live, we called to find a priest to administer last rites. Andy indicated to me that he was comfortable, refusing any further medications for pain or anxiety, but his breathing sounded awful. It was this loud, rasping sound, as if his airway were obstructed. Every breath was labored. There was nothing to do but wait.

Katie pulled on my arm, and asked if we could talk. She pulled me into her bedroom and closed the door. Once inside, I looked into the eyes of my step-daughter and saw intense pain. She burst into tears and kept repeating, "I don't know what to do. I don't know what to do." I thought I understood her. I told her that I didn't know either, that we would face it together, that we would hold her Dad's hand until he stopped breathing, that he was dying now and that he needed to concentrate on Jesus. She listened well, but urged me further. "No" she said. "He's alive because of me. I feel like he's staying here because of me, and I don't want him to do that. I want him to go now." She had watched only a few minutes of his suffering to take breaths, and she couldn't bear it any longer. She asked me if she could talk to him. I told her that she could and that we would clear the room for her to do so.

When everyone else had left, I woke Andy up. I spoke loudly so that he couldn't stay asleep. I told him Katie needed to talk to him. She looked at me for confirmation that she should really do this, I nodded. Andy looked at her through labored breaths as she spoke. She did not cry. She didn't stammer. She bravely spoke up. She said, "Dad, it's okay if you need to go now. I will be okay. I will stay in school, and I will do well. I will make you proud of me. I promise. I will graduate. I will remember all that you taught me. It is okay for you to go now. Don't stay here just for me. Catherine will take care of me." She hugged him then. Through weak arms, he hugged her back. She cried on his chest for a short while, and we asked everyone back into the room.

It was then, I suppose that Andy made the decision to move on from this home into the next. Within the hour, after the priest had come by and after Matthew and Corinne came in to say goodbye, while soft music played, he died. As Andy drew his last breath, his expression made Katie smile and giggle a tiny bit. I worried that one day she would regret that laugh, that she would worry that it was insensitive, but I have done my best to convince her that things happened just as they were supposed to. Andy was meant to hear Katie's laughter as the last sound on earth before he left us. It was meant to be that way.

I can't imagine the feeling of being caught between both homes that way. Knowing the way that

Andy wanted to care for Katie, and the way in which he knew the Lord and wanted to be with Him too, makes the picture clearer.   Our will to live does matter.

35

HOW DID THIS HAPPEN?

"How did this happen?"

I used to ask Andy that question regularly when we were first dating.

I'd get a wave of the reminder that he had been 'just the social studies teacher across the hall' and I'd get scared. I'd look at him and truly want the answer to the question, "How did this happen?" I wanted to know how we went from colleagues to lovers. I wanted to know how it felt like there were two Andy's: the one I'd known in school and the one I'd gotten to know personally.

He responded in many ways. (I asked the question a lot.) Sometimes I got a little smile, sometimes a laugh. Sometimes he'd actually try for an answer, like,

"This was part of the plan" or "I don't know, but I'm glad it did."

When Andy and I got married after almost two years of dating, I went through the same transition. After the wedding, I needed some time to question. "How did this happen?" Andy was wonderful about it. He was so patient with my worries and fears. He waited. I felt like he understood me better than I understood myself. He knew my story and how hard it was for me to trust. Eventually, the questioning subsided. I settled in to the idea that God had given us an incredible gift. I was head-over-heals in love with someone who was wonderfully good to me. I respected him, admired him, and adored him. He was interesting, smart, thoughtful, and funny. The best part was that he actually loved me, too. I couldn't believe that we were fortunate enough to have found people we loved and discovered that the feelings were completely reciprocated. Many people in the world never find this. Some are not quite sure if it exists at all. It does exist, and it left me wondering. "How did this happen?"

When Andy died just three years after we were married, I really wanted to know. "How did *this* happen?" Andy wasn't here for me to ask. I guess he never had a real answer anyway. We aren't privy to that kind of information. God doesn't run things past us before he plans out our lives. And deaths.

It's hard to sit like a philosopher and wrap this all up neatly, but I can say that I understand God has given me free will. He has put my life in motion and allowed me to make decisions. Some have been good. Some have been disastrous. We like to take credit for the decisions that turn out well. We like to pass off the blame of the not-so-good ones onto other people, or to fate or to God. If God is in it, He's in all of them. So then, do things *happen* to us?

I have to trust that God is in all of our happenings. Here in this situation, where my spiritual partner, my lover, my friend was taken from me, I can only manage it with trust. I trust God. I know that if Andy is not here, it is because God has a plan for us to be apart now. If I can trust Him when things go my way and praise Him when it all works out, then I can do the same when I wish circumstances were different. Who better to trust than God himself? He has given life. I've witnessed it and experienced it. He also takes away.

"How did this happen?"

God allowed it. He knows what's best for me. I trust Him. "It is well with my soul."

Please don't misunderstand this. *I am very sad.* I cry more than I ever believed a person could cry, with a voice I've never heard before. I hear this sound coming from the pit of my stomach, I think. It's me. It's sorrow. It's anguish. It's a feeling of despair triggered by this catastrophic loss in my life. When I say that I cry, I really do cry. I may have peace about Andy's passing because I trust God, but it in no way takes away the pain of mourning. Every activity, every moment, every song, every meal, every laugh is accompanied by pain for me. It is not the same without my partner. Truly, though, I can't imagine what it must be like for someone who doesn't trust God. The anger, the hurt, the blaming: I'm relieved that those are not the emotions I'm handling. I guess that means that I do know how this happened...or maybe that I'm content *not* to know, but to trust that God does.

36

THE D'ANGELO FAMILY A YEAR LATER

Subject: The D'Angelo Family a Year Later...
Date: April 16, 2009

Thursday, April 16th, marks a full year since Andy died.

Yes, that did go fast -- and it was torturously slow, too.

So, how have we fared over the year? Have we been strong? Have we forged ahead? I don't know about all of that, but I do know that I have learned to celebrate smaller victories, like rising out of bed each morning, taking a shower, and getting to work. I have learned to let the dishes sit while I listen to the kind of day my kids had and take the time to go for a walk when the weather's nice. You never know what kind of day tomorrow will be.

I reflect on the last year -- and the one before it -- and marvel at the truth of what has really happened. I stand in amazement of what God must think of me. Y'know what I mean? We all have heard it said: "God never gives us more than we can handle." Well, God must think I'm pretty tough, then. The trials we've seen have been DOOZIES!

Yet, here I am a year later. I've changed a few things: added an apartment to help pay the bills, bought a cocker spaniel puppy to add life to our Christmas, changed my hair -- and added music to my daily life. I have always had a song in my heart, but now it is purposeful. Music has changed our house. Corinne has become more serious about her clarinet and is taking up piano. Matthew is 'BEAST' on the guitar (his 13-year-old lingo, not mine). I have been committed to practicing my clarinet and piano, and singing my HEAD OFF... and hoping to take up harmonica this year. Katie brought her keyboard and guitar up to Albany to practice more there. All of us have found comfort in music. So, we continue.

Over the year I've cried out to God on many occasions with a sound I've never heard before, and I want to know why I'm still here. I haven't really felt like it. I haven't understood why God would unite two people spiritually and then take one of them out of the game. It's made me say that I don't want to play anymore. It's a new feeling for me.

Then, I just continue. I keep going anyway. I don't know why I'm here. I don't know why Andy's not. I don't understand why there are flowers and blades of grass that are able to grow up out of the driveway either. I just trust God that He knows what is best for us. I also trust God that His promise to be with me through it all is true. And He has been with me. I have never been alone through these days -- even when the crying comes from somewhere I can't imagine exists and the sound is unfamiliar to me. I just keep going. With a song in my heart, I just keep going.

Thank you, Lord, for being my strength. Thank you for carrying me through a tough year. I trust You that I will continue to be carried as I need it. Lord, help me through the next days as I am reminded of the loss. Help me to count my blessings.

I'm headed to work on a day that I thought I couldn't do it. I'm planning to spend as much time in my classroom as I can muster. Pray for me. Ask God to keep a song in my heart that will lift my spirit as I attempt something that feels impossible. It smells like spring, and the flowers remind me of a funeral. Pray for me.

Some of you will be at the 11:30 mass at the Shrine in Manorville today. All are invited to attend. God bless you all. Thank you for sharing a few minutes with me. :)

~Catherine D'Angelo

37

SUSTAINING LIFE

When I taught first grade in Christian school back in 2002-03, I was given the daily challenge of teaching Bible lessons. It was difficult for me, having never taught Bible lessons before. I took the curriculum with its mini-lessons and scripture references and activity choices and ran with it. It was fun. I learned a lot about the Bible that I wouldn't have had the chance to learn otherwise.

I thought that I was blessing the children when I came out with witty ideas and stories. I may have been, but I was really the one being blessed by God at the same time. Often, I'd find myself answering a student's curiosities with words of wisdom I don't really have. I truly felt as if God were speaking through me and to me. It was amazing to feel as though Jesus, the teacher, was teaching me. I laughed to myself many

times as I spoke out words to students as if I understood it all – and I bet six-year-olds believed that I was
wise. I was being prepared to listen, though. I had
to be prepared for the blessings that were to come. If
I hadn't learned to hear what God was saying and to
speak it out, then I would have missed what God had
planned for my life next.

During the week before Easter, the children's lessons were naturally centered around the Passion. I
had a particularly hard time with teaching six-year-
olds about beatings and brutality and crucifixion. I
know how important it is that we not ignore the severity of the sacrifice God the Father and Jesus made for
us, but I was concerned about how to teach it with sen-
sitivity to their developmental stage. In short, I didn't
want to scare the pants off of them.

So, my lessons skimmed around the edges of the
death itself. I tried to focus on the Last Supper and
the events around it. I talked about Jesus needing to
pray in the Garden of Gethsemane. I talked about
the loyalty of the disciples. I taught them all of this
through a skit that they planned to perform for the
entire pre-K through 12th grade student body at
chapel service. Our parents made costumes. Video
cameras rolled. It was a big hit, but it was more than
that.

As was typical, I wound up teaching myself something. While assigning parts for the skit, I found that none of the students wanted to play Judas. They were sure that Judas was the reason that our beautiful Savior had suffered and died. In the estimation of a six-year-old, when something bad happens, there is always someone to blame. I think adults struggle with that, too.

In the interest of not letting our little Judas (played by an almost unwilling Zachary) feel like an outcast to his first-grade friends, I tried to take the heat off of Judas. Again, though, God was working through the kids to teach me a valuable lesson, one that I'd need to take with me through the death of my husband.

I sat all of my kids down and made a chart on our blackboard. I questioned them, asking each of them who we should blame for Jesus dying. Most said Judas. Some said Satan. Then someone offered that the Sanhedrin was at fault. Someone blamed the arresting soldiers. They were searching for the right answer. They were looking to me to tell them the right answer. Is there a right answer?

It ended with God taking over. I felt directed by the Holy Spirit as I told the kids that none of those listed on the board were to blame. I told them that *God* had made the decision to bring Jesus to the cross. I told them that the Lord had allowed people to behave in certain ways to further His divine plan. I told them that Judas had to turn Jesus in. "Someone had to," I said, "so that Jesus could die for our sins." I quickly pointed out that even Jesus was not mad at Judas. He didn't put up a fight. He didn't allow others to fight for him. He continued to behave in God's gentle peace and love. What a powerful message.

They were so cute. They sat with open mouths contemplating the idea that Judas may not be a bad guy after all. Maybe he was used by God for a mighty cause. Maybe the soldiers were meant to arrest Jesus. Maybe Pontius Pilate was not the executioner that they thought he was. They thought about it for a moment; then they asked me if it was snack time. Of course it was. Who can contemplate life's big questions without breaking for a snack? Over snack, the chatter was blameless, and little Zachary could hold his head high again as he played Judas.

I say that I learned that lesson with my first graders, but did I really? When it came time for me to accept the will of the Lord in Andy's death, did I just happily grab a snack and move on like they did?

When I watched a man who seemed quite alive one year prior whither before my eyes and doubt about his chances of living, did I just accept it as God's will? It's hard to accept that Andy died because it was his time to die.

I've watched my plants wither and die. I see them hanging on – even when I forget to water them. I see them pull away from the sun, or turn toward the sun in search of what they need to live, but mostly, I have really had little success with house plants. They are meant to live outside where the rain can water them when I forget.

Then again, I've looked at the hearty plants, too. I've watched the tiger lilies and the roses and the hydrangea outside in the yard. I see the grape vine come up from nothing every year. I see these plants hibernate for the colder seasons and then burst with life again in the spring and summer. I watch this and think of Andy. How can it be that some things live and some things die? What is it that makes the difference? I'm new to gardening, and I'm trying to educate myself. I feel that if my plants die, it's because of some negligence on my part. I try to figure out what that is so that next time my plants will live long enough to produce the fruit I'd hoped for. It's tough to do when you're a busy working Mom of three. I forgive myself when I have to turn over or rip out another shriveled plant. It's a shame, but it's just a plant. I can try again next year, right?

Not so with people. I watched Andy just die. He just died. I did everything that I could do: the best doctors and then more doctors and then more doctors, medicines and natural remedies, prayer together, prayer alone, meditation, prayer from others, music, research, diet, supplements, etc. I tried everything I could. In the end, all I could do was hold him and pray with him and love him and care for him. Isn't that beautiful? Why, yes, but that is not what I had intended. I wasn't planning to write this ending or to learn these lessons. I was planning to have a testimonial at the end of this story where we could sit hand in hand and sing the praises to God for Andy's miraculous healing. We could talk about how hard those months had been and know that they were behind us. We could laugh at that enemy of a devil who tried to take him down with cancer, but failed. Instead, I had to watch him die and plan a funeral.

I can't understand it really. How does God decide who lives or dies? My 12-year son put it well one day on the way to school. I was reminding him to pray for Andy again that morning. I was telling him the details of some appointment about which we were feeling hopeful. We were praying for answers from God on how to proceed. I wanted everyone around us to pray. Then Matthew said, "Hey, Mom? Do you think God is up in Heaven counting how many prayers come in about Andy? Do you think he has a running total or something? Like he's saying, 'Wow! Andy got the most prayers, I guess I have to heal *him* today!'?"

I was stumped. I couldn't answer that. Of course I don't think that God is a God of wishes, but didn't it sound like I was asking God to grant a wish when I asked Matthew to pray that day? I guess it did. It seemed that way to me suddenly, too. What is the purpose of prayer if we can't have the answer that we want? Sounds like a simple question. A twelve-year-old is good to have around at times like this.

So, "Who is to blame for Andy's death?" Strong faith reminds me that God's will is always at work. I trust God that He wouldn't do what isn't best for all of us. I do not understand God's will here. I want to be with Andy. I miss him. I want him here with me or me there with him. I don't like being separated, so I want God to have other plans. He doesn't have other plans, though. He made *this* decision. Andy is not with me now. I could blame myself, like I do with the plants. I could blame the doctors. I could blame the system that should have found a cure to cancer by now, or believe the conspiracy that the cure isn't being revealed to us because of big business and money issues. It's just that none of that really matters. It is so already. Andy isn't here. It's like the Judas story. It's not about blame. In fact, the point is not worth pondering. We are not given all of the answers. We are asked to 'trust in the Lord with all our heart and lean not on our own understanding.'

So, here I go, Lord. No leaning. I'm standing straight up, looking at you to direct me. I know, Lord, that I hate living without Andy, but I trust you that you know better than I do. I am so very, very sad about the loss in our lives. I am confused by what direction to take. I am feeling impatient about having to wait to see Andy again, but I know that I will.

As for Matthew's question, I did come up with an answer. (*Thank you, Lord for giving me more insight.*) I told him that we don't pray with a list of requests. That is what children do when they believe Santa is bringing them gifts. God is bigger than that. God does take requests, but why would we begin to tell God what's best for us? Shouldn't He know that already?

So, why pray, then?

The reason is that we really need to have a *relationship* with God. We really need to know Him. We have to cry with Him, sing to Him, praise His name. It is in that relationship that comfort comes. We can feel confident in little else. God is always there.

I told Matthew that we were storming Heaven with prayer so that He could see how important Andy is to us. God sees our contrition, our humility, our selflessness. He sees our compassion and our love for Andy. We show God how we are growing. What parent isn't pleased when their child matures to the point of *relationship*? I hope that was enough of an answer for Matthew. As the days got harder and we didn't have our prayers answered, I hope that the thought of relationship to God was enough to keep him going.

Children look to their Moms for answers. I really wanted to sustain Matthew with the right answers, just like with my first-graders on Easter. I wanted to find the right inspired words that would be enough to carry him through. I prayed that God would do what I could not. I didn't know any better than a twelve-year-old did about prayer and God's motivation for how He spins our world. I had been in much the same position as Matthew, waiting on God, fearful that the worst would happen, praying for relief, holding on in preparation in case things didn't go well. I didn't know then how to sustain my son in a time of questioning.

I am still faced with the challenge of sustaining life. My husband has passed, and there are children to care for, plants in the garden, plants in the kitchen, a dog, a cat, a rabbit….and oh….the chickens. I've had trouble with chickens.

I remember our first spring living in Manorville. Andy agreed to let me hatch chickens from their eggs using an incubator in our kitchen. I was so excited about it! I couldn't wait to see their little faces and hear their little, "Peep, peeps." I thought this was going to be so cool. We took the kids to visit other friends of ours who had done the same in their homes. They had full-grown chickens to prove it! They even got eggs daily.

Andy and I researched this, as good teachers always do when they take on projects. We looked up plans for building our own chicken coop online. We got library books on raising chickens. We made plans to have them free range all day to eat any bugs in our yard. (What a bonus! Manorville, Long Island, where we live, is riddled with ticks, some of which carry Lyme disease. Wouldn't it be great to avoid spraying pesticides by having the hens eat their way through the yard daily to keep us tick-free?)

The kids had a blast waiting for life to pop out before our eyes. Who am I kidding? I think I may have had more fun than they did! It's a good thing, too, because the daily chore of cleaning up after and feeding the chickens became my sole responsibility. It was a lot of work. When they were living in the house, I had to vacuum up after them as they flapped their baby wings in the little box they called home. The mashed corn that they eat is a fine powder. It stuck to everything like volcanic ash. I had to do this every day. I also had to keep a heat lamp on them. I had to feed them and clean up their water feeder after they pooped right on it. Still cute?

Eventually, the chicks moved in to the coop that Andy and I had bickered about building correctly. It was quite an improvement to have them out of the house and out of the vegetable garden, too. They were free-ranging and eating bugs as planned. We made sure they had water, closed the henhouse door at night…oops…did I forget to close the door tonight?... awww….nothing will happen to them tonight….what is that noise?....is that the dog?....she must hear something outside…." Yeah. That's how it went. All of our chickens were slowly picked off in this manner. Because we live in the woods essentially, there are predatory night animals like foxes and possums and raccoons that love to eat chickens. One wrong move, and I'm responsible for the death of another one of my cute little egg-laying babies.

That's how it went. One by one, all of our chickens fell prey to the night. Now we have none. Ain't that just the circle of life?

On the day after that first raid of the chicken coop, I was so mad at Mother Nature that I couldn't even go in my garden. I didn't want to keep my bargain with my plants to care for them. I felt that part of nature had betrayed me. I felt tricked by nature.

Strangely, that's exactly how I felt about Andy's illness. Remember, I felt used by God. Used. Really used. I felt cheated and tricked by death or life or nature or whatever, but I was upset. How could this have happened to me again and again? The house plants, the chickens, now my husband? *What next, Lord? What?*

It made more sense than I realized to hear "I'll Follow the Sun" on the morning of Andy's wake. I think I had forgotten how mad I felt at the sun. I know that's just stupid, to target the sun in my anger: a celestial, inanimate being. It was unavoidable, though. Day after day as I had been struggling through the gravity of Andy's illness, living with the threat that nothing in my life could be normal again, I looked at the sun with disdain, as though it were simply disrespectful for continuing to come up each day. It just moved through our sky as our world turned through another day. Days kept coming, without regard for the loss we were expecting. I had always looked at the sun as if it were smiling down on us. Now, I felt like it should stop smiling. "How rude! My husband is sick! How can you just stay up there smiling like nothing is wrong?! Everything is wrong!" Still, the sun came up again. Every day, the sun came up again. Every single day. No regard for loss. I truly felt it would have been respectful for the sun to bow in mourning, for the sun to stop shining so brightly out of respect for Andy. Guess what? That didn't happen, and it made me feel as though we were just inconsequential in this giant world, kind of like the feeling I get when I stand on the shore by the ocean. I feel small, really small. I get that full experience of being very, very small in this big, giant world. I feel how big our God is then, too. It's a great place to stand in humility and pray.

In this case, though, where I was actually yelling and sneering at the sun, I was not in a place of humility. I was in a place of, "How dare you!?" at God. Who am I to address our Creator that way? I had lost sight of the role that I am meant to play in God's created world. I felt entitled to God's continued blessing and even his reverence in ordering the sun to back off when my husband was battling for his life. Wow. Ever feel that way? Entitled to order God to do as you see fit? Putting it on paper brings things into perspective.

Holding Andy's hand as he took his last breaths brought me back to my proper place as clay, not potter. I have absolutely no power over life or death. I really did know this all along. Somewhere I had gotten caught up in myself and forgotten.

When I consider the giant chore of sustaining life, whether it be plants or pets or children or sick husbands, it reminds me of when my first-graders wanted me to figure out who was to blame for death. The discussions seem at first to be very different, but I see the same message: we are free of responsibility over life and death.

There is a freedom in trusting God and allowing His capable arms to sustain us and love us, fully relaxing in the knowledge that He is in charge of our lives and our deaths, but, it can be frightening, too. It can mean that even though God gives us work to do here on earth, like feeding pets and watering plants and nurturing children, we truly have very little power.

Thankfully, the Lord is trustworthy. I pray to build on that trust relationship. I can tell the Lord my deepest thoughts. I can ask questions. He knows me already, too. I can whisper my hopes and fears. He cherishes them and never uses them against me. He protects me from true harm with His continual comfort and love, while still having me go through trials that would otherwise truly be harmful. He gives me peace with his presence and guidance. His Holy Spirit speaks to me gently and patiently, even when I am stubborn. I know that I am loved and not alone. I feel a calm, warm, constant nurturing from the Lord.

He is my Eternal Father, my Creator, and my Friend. I am blessed to have such a trusting relationship.

The lesson for us is about trusting God's perfect will. Sounds simple, but makes me feel the need for a snack break.

38

NOTICING THE DECOR

It had been almost two years after Andy passed when I was sitting on the couch in my psychologist's office and noticed that the doctor had redecorated. Dr. Quilty paused and smiled slightly, a look of calm surprise on his face. He then told me that he hadn't redecorated in the entire time I'd been coming to him for grief counseling. His office hadn't changed at all. I felt foolish, scanning the room again. Surely, he must be mistaken. I felt like this was my first time seeing everything. I laughed at myself nervously and said, "You got *some* new things, right?"

Again, a gentle "No" and a shake of his head. He explained then that it was a sign of healing for me to begin noticing my surroundings. He said that grieving patients are often so very centered on their own personal issues and the little bitty circle of their own life that they overlook their daily surroundings. My beginning to take notice of the decor in the office I'd been in each month was progress then.

Other areas of my life reflected this truth about grieving, too. There was too much to handle. I could manage myself: showers, some laundry, some meals, putting gas in the car. I forgot appointments and conversations, though. I lost things. I ignored mail. I left things at home that I needed at work. I left things at work that I needed at home. I missed deadlines. I just couldn't focus as I needed to, as I used to be able to do. It's strange, but at the time I didn't consider this to be a symptom of grieving; I attributed it to the absence of Andy in my life. I felt as though him not being there to help me remember or take up some of the slack as my life partner was what had me all disheveled. I was wrong.

Yes, I missed Andy's help. I missed having someone to discuss my life with and make plans with at the end of each day, but that is not what I'm getting at here. What I'm saying is that grief itself causes a strange kind of limited vision. As a symptom of the brokenhearted loss I was experiencing, I narrowed my focus to myself first, then my household family, then slowly, I was able to pan out until one day I recognized common decor as brand new.

Just as I was surprised to find that I truly liked the way Dr. Quilty's office was decorated, I was also surprised to find how my children had been grieving. Now, Katie, the oldest of the kids, and away at school, had been a worry and a concern of mine from the start. I knew that Andy had taken exceptional care to make sure she felt loved and felt special. Without him here to keep that up, I worried for her. I distinctly remember Andy asking me to make sure she was okay. "Take care of Katie, even if she won't let you," he told me. "Take care of my daughter." I really wanted to honor that agreement. I was by her side throughout the illness and in all of our grieving days. My vision panned out quickly to include her in my little circle right from the beginning.

When I say that I was surprised to find my own children grieving, I mean my children from my first marriage, Matthew and Corinne who had a stepfather in Andy. We all expected Katie to need support and comfort, and we knew that Matthew and Corinne had experienced a great loss, too, but I guess I was surprised to find out how hard it would really be.

Each of them handled the loss differently. They were both sad and cried at times, but they looked as though they felt an obligation to be strong for me, the one who usually could hold them together. They both missed Andy and how he added to our household.

They just showed their sorrow differently. Their grieving certainly didn't look anything like my own did, so
it was hard to figure out how to help.

When Matthew needed time and space to grieve,
he played basketball and guitar. He did that most of
the time. In fact, I wouldn't have been surprised if he
fell asleep at night with a guitar in his grip. He cried,
too. When he was sad, he would walk away from me or
retreat to his room and just cry.

Corinne was different. She held it in, forcing smiles
when she felt upset, complaining of stomach aches that
kept her from eating and her usual type-A personality diligence in school. She was in the nurse's office
literally every day. God bless those school nurses who
allowed her to just sit there instead of in her classroom.
She lost a lot of weight in that first year, so much so
that I headed to doctors for testing, all to prove what
we all suspected: she was grieving, too.

I was forced to ask a lot of them in those early days.
That made it harder, I imagine. With Katie away at
college, it left only the three of us at home. They witnessed the raw upset of my grieving up close and could
do nothing about it. I would be cooking dinner and
stop in my tracks, sit cross-legged on the kitchen floor
and cry, or they would watch me in the morning try to
put make-up on over the swollen, Rocky Balboa eyes

that I would get from crying in my sleep. I tried to trim our schedule to include only church, stopping music lessons and dancing school and most of our social activity. None of us felt like going out anyway. I think that I made good choices about that, but it wasn't enough to stop the flood of upset that came anyway.

I worry that the hardest part for them was not having me to lean on. I had been forcing myself to go on with life. The really important details like getting to work and staying there all day doing a good job as a happy teacher took their toll. By the end of the day, when the sun was kind enough to go down and the evening was setting in, I would feed the kids quickly and urge them to get to bed. I knew that I had to cry, that I had been holding it in all day and that I could not hold it in any longer. Although they definitely saw my tears and they noticed the change in me, saw me grieving, I really tried not to lose it, really *lose it* when they were around and awake. I needed them to get to bed, even if it were earlier than their usual bedtime. Unfortunately, children usually don't operate on the schedule of their parents or consider that they might have feelings and needs of their own.

From the very start of parenthood, we learn this lesson. Babies cry. They cry at night when we're trying to sleep. They cry during dinner when we're trying to eat. They cry in the store when we're trying to shop. They cry in the car when we're trying to get somewhere. They want their needs met immediately: Basic Parenting 101.

Our job is to teach them not to behave selfishly. We hope they learn this as they grow. We teach them that they must wait their turn. Maybe a younger sibling is born or a little cousin is around whose needs must be met first. Kindergarten teachers and others help with those early lessons in delaying gratification. Somehow, though, my kids never did get the memo that all of those lessons apply even at bedtime. For them, when I am tired and ready to turn in for the night, it has no bearing on whether or not their day is over. They have one more thing to tell me about, one more question to ask, one more thing they've forgotten to talk over with me. "And Mom, where is my....?" "Don't forget to call so-and-so's Mom tomorrow." "I have this itchy patch on my shoulder." Whatever it is, it must be attended to immediately. Both of my kids do this. In fact, they especially like doing it at the same time!

The bedtime ritual in my house had always been difficult for me. It was in those moments that I usually gave in completely to their requests to have their back scratched or a story read to them or a boo-boo re-inspected. On most days, my fatigue would win over and I'd fall asleep in one of their beds trying to listen to their every need up until the very last second of my day. I love them. I complain about all of that, but I never made an effort to change it. I had the foresight to see that it would absolutely have an ending. Those days are so very short in a child' s life, the days when they want their mom to hang out in their bedroom before sleep. I made an effort to indulge them in this nightly ritual, even though it could get tiresome and frustrating.

So, Matthew and Corinne had grown accustomed to the pattern I had established early on in their lives that I could be pushed at bedtime. I could be stretched to listen more, to spend the extra minute, to give in one more time. That pattern changed during our days of grieving. I couldn't be around them. I couldn't be patient for another second. I had to get to my room and close the door. I had to. I needed to cry. I had to be alone. I had to. I needed to write, to call out to God or Andy or the air in our bedroom. I had to. No one could witness it. No one could be a part of it. No one could be awake in the house for it. I had to cry. I had to.

Their patient Mom transformed into a frantic, up-set ball of un-shed tears. I looked them deep in the eyes and told them they must go to bed. They must stay in their rooms. They must not call out for me or come knock on my door. I told them flat out that I had been holding in the tears all day, and I couldn't hold them in another second. I felt the welling within me. I heard it in my voice as I urgently spoke to them. I told them I loved them, kissed them each goodnight and marched to my room. I closed the door. I locked it. I was off-limits to my kids, something I had never been before.

Grieving is emotional, gut-wrenching work. When I peek into my journals from those days, I become absorbed in the pain all over again. To say loss is difficult or that sorrow is painful is just not getting to the core of it. This pain created a change in me. I can't see things the way I did before. I am changed.

Can you remember back to when you were a small child and you were denied something you really wanted? Something you really felt you should have? Something you were entitled to? Maybe something you had your hopes on getting? I can. It's not that I'm remembering one specific thing; I'm remembering the feeling of being denied. Maybe my Mom said I couldn't have something at the grocery store or denied permission for an activity I had my heart set on already. Whatever it may have been, I remember the feeling of really wanting something I could not have. For me, that's a root feeling for grief.

I am now denied access to someone I love, someone who loves me, too and is part of me. I am denied his attention and his smile and the smell of his face and hair. I am denied his humor and the giggle that went with it. I am denied his opinion and his insight. I am denied his intellect and his sarcasm. I am denied his company and his warm touch, his kisses and his snoring on the pillow beside me. Like a small, spoiled child, I wanted to stomp my feet in frustration in an attempt to have Andy back. There is no one to petition here, though. Reason and intelligence dictate that people don't return from the grave on this side of heaven. I knew that. I knew he couldn't return. I knew I had to figure out how to go on without him, too. I had to choose to either live without him or to join him in death.

I know the people who loved me saw this truth: that I wasn't sure whether I could live like this without him. The fastest way to get to him was for me to just die, too. I also knew that I couldn't do that to my family. If it hadn't been for my children, I can't say that I wouldn't have considered ending my life. I couldn't find other reasons to stay here when the biggest love of my life was now in Heaven.

The kids gave me reasons to clean the house, pay the bills, stay focussed enough at work to not lose my job, to get there every day and earn my paycheck. They gave me reasons to shop for food and cook again, even if I couldn't eat. They gave me reasons to smile, too, and they gave me the only reason I could find to agree to stay here on earth instead of rush toward Andy.

I had been wildly busy before this grieving began. For the five months of pancreatic cancer, one month of cardiac healing, and additional week of healing from shoulder surgery, I cared for a grown man night and day. I hadn't been sleeping like I needed to sleep for over six months. I was often awakened to the sound of vomiting or to Andy's need to talk and his inability to sleep. I was awakened by my own upset about how many, many things needed to be done and remembered. I had lists by my bedside on days that I remembered to keep them. I whimpered through anxiety dreams on nights that I had forgotten to.

So, when the funeral had passed and all of those responsibilities had been removed, it was a big and sudden change, a halt in the action.

The kids handled that halt better than I did, I think. They started playing this game called FOUR SQUARE, apparently a common playground game. My kids played by using sidewalk chalk to draw boxes on the pavement in our road. They stood inside the boxes and used a ball to try to get each other out in a dodge-ball kind of way, I think. I really still don't know. I did know that they had been laughing with our neighbors and fellow Monday Night kids in front of the house on our dead end street. Sometimes they were on scooters, sometimes they were on bikes or played basketball, but lately, they just played four square.

After a few days of my staring off into nothing and crying instead of eating, I heard my children laughing in the road. I knew they were out there, but I guess I didn't hear it until then. I had been satisfied that they were content and letting me have some time, but when I heard them, really *heard* them, I put on my sneakers and went out to play, too. It was hard to see them laughing. I knew they needed to, and so did I, but it was hard to imagine anything that could conjure up a laugh when life had just taken such an awful turn for us, when we still had funeral flowers on the front lawn. This time, as the sun peeked through the woods that surround our house, I followed their lead.

My kids were happy to see me outside and eager to share their game with me. I sat on the curb next to Delilah, our faithful black Labrador who always stood by when they played in the road, but I could see that my presence was ruining the game a bit. They had been playing and bickering over who made what shot and who was playing fairly. My being there made them pause before business as usual. Maybe they felt it was irreverent to just keep playing, my swollen face as the outward reminder that our home was filled with sadness. Instead of ruining their fun, I saw it as an opportunity to teach them, even if I were actually teaching myself at the same time, that grieving must include living, too.

I stood up from the curb and asked about the rules. They all started explaining the rules to me at the same time, as only excited kids can do. They were smiling and relieved to see me up from the curb, happy to see their Mom trying to come back from somewhere they couldn't really understand. We didn't discuss one word of all that, choosing instead to focus on the game and the fun.

A funny thing happened then, Judi came out from her house to join us in one of the squares. My parents came over and watched our silly game. My brother came over and he and his wife took a turn, too. And we laughed. We played and we laughed. It turns out that not much has changed since I was a little girl, I still stink at playground games, and my kids laughed all the more because of it. That game was the entrance into living again for us. It was the permission we gave ourselves to laugh again.

39

THANK YOU

Subject: Thank You
Date: April, 2010

Dear Friends,

It has been nearly two years since Andy died.

He influences some of us still. I've gotten calls and emails from many of you saying that Andy has made himself present in your lives. He was in the hot-tempered presidential debates. He was in the prompting to call me when I was sad. He was even called 'the angel in the outfield' when his beloved Yankees won the Series last fall. He is not here to look at or to touch, but he seems to tell the radio DJ's when to play a Beatles song, doesn't he? Well, whether he does or he doesn't, it is true that many of us have felt him in our hearts and minds and dreams and that we have prayed for his soul.

I am writing today so that I can finally thank you, as is the formal custom for all that you did during Andy's illness and throughout the mourning period. I wrote out these Thank You cards a few days after Andy passed and could never bring myself to send them. I guess it was in the sending that I would see finality. I know it sounds silly, but I wasn't ready to do that. So, they sat on our bookshelf for almost two years. (Sorry if they're a little dusty!) Healing comes in so many forms; I've learned to question less and accept grief and healing as they come.

I want you all to know that my intent was to write a personal note in each card and tell you that I truly was touched by each act of kindness and each gift and each call or prayer. I noticed all of it, even in the turmoil. I noticed how you ALL came together to grieve with us and love us. I will never forget that.

I also want to send a note of encouragement. We felt so assured that our faith was enough to carry us through, but we lost Andy anyway. Weren't our prayers strong enough? Was our faith weak?

Let me share something I learned recently that straightened this out for me. There is a passage in the Bible that reminds us of the people in our old Bible stories whose faith was strong -- stronger than we could ever boast. The faith of Abel, Noah, Abraham, Sarah, Isaac, Jacob, Joseph, Moses, and David are mentioned. We know their stories. We are reminded that, "...all these people were still living by faith when they died. They did not receive the things promised; they only saw them and welcomed them from a distance." (Hebrews 11:13)

Faith is described here as, "...being sure of what we hope for and certain of what we do not see." Andy and I felt this kind of faith all around us during his illness. We didn't just trust God because we thought He was a wish-granting genie. We didn't love Him because of that either. In the absence of answered prayers, God doesn't stop being God. We still love Him and trust Him.

We also saw this faith coming from Andy's students. You may have noticed that there were folded origami paper cranes at Andy's wake. We put them in baskets. We strung them around the room. We placed some on the tables in handfuls. There were 1,000 of them, hand-folded by the students of Shelter Island School. The Junior High read a story about a girl who became deathly ill after the bombs were dropped on Japan. The story, called, "One Thousand Paper Cranes," doesn't end well. The girl and her friends fold paper cranes in an effort to save her life by reaching their goal of 1,000. They fold and fold, but the girl dies anyway.

Just like in that story, we did all that we could do, too. As George Harrison said, "All things must pass away."

Tonight, I put each beautifully-folded and student-signed crane into my fireplace. I watched the vibrant colors burn up as I prayed for each child that hoped and folded in pure faith. I pray for you all that your faith remains as strong, even when we do not receive what we hope for.

May God bless you and your families as you have blessed ours.

With love and affection and gratitude,

~Catherine D'Angelo and family

40

JOB

Do you know who Job is? I thought I did. Trials. I always thought the story of Job was about trials. It is about trials. I thought it was about a faithful man in whom God was well-pleased. I thought it was about the testing of his faith, about how God allowed Satan to test him to make a point. And it *is* about that, but, I missed some things along the way. It's also about faith and humility and righteousness. I learned a lot about Job through this experience. I'm still learning.

In the summer of 2007, my son Matthew was injured playing football. He broke two bones in his foot: emergency room visit, x-rays, crutches. A week or so later, Andy had shoulder surgery: hospital stay, pain meds, stitches. Six days later, Andy had a heart attack: ambulance ride, terrifying brush with death, long recovery. Six weeks later, I had a bad mammogram: ultrasound, biopsy, visit with surgeon. Days later, Andy was diagnosed with pancreatic cancer. In the middle of all of this, we had mounting bills, a daughter in college, a huge mortgage, and the start of my tenure year teaching. My Dad chuckled as he spoke out what many were probably thinking, "Job has nothing on you two." He said it to lighten the mood, as my Dad likes to do, but to also point out the severity of the many trials we were suddenly facing. These were not little disturbances. Even facing just one of those circumstances would have been upsetting. All of them at once was too much.

Usually, I am a terrific sleeper. I can fall asleep anywhere. My Mom loves to marvel that I can close my eyes and in a minute or two, I will be asleep. Sleeping is actually one of my favorite things to do. I even fell asleep on that first date with Andy. It's part of what made that night perfect for us. We slept. It was amazing. Suddenly, though, I was robbed of my ability to sleep. I was continually reminded of that line in Macbeth, "Glamis has murdered sleep!" Add that to the list of things that kept me awake. One night, I gave up and crept downstairs quietly, curled up on our couch in the wee hours of the morning, and instead of sleeping, grabbed the Bible and read. I wasn't sure what I would read. Truly, I wanted something boring to help me sleep, even if it meant falling out on the couch instead of my bed. I thought about what my Dad had said and turned to the book of Job. I knew the premise that God allowed Job to be tested and then realized that I didn't know how it ended. I got a little excited thinking that maybe it would have a happy ending. "Maybe the trials in my life will end as they must have for Job. Maybe the happy ending will be in my life, too."

I got very tired as I read. I wanted to close my eyes and finally sleep, but I wanted more to find the peace that I was sure would be at the end of the book. I knew that reading a happy ending would settle me into a peaceful sleep, again back in a position of strong faith. After all, reading the Bible is supposed to help us, right? Surely, I would be rewarded for my efforts here. God would see me diligently searching for hope and insight. Unfortunately, Job is not a short book. There are 42 chapters to the book of Job. So, I stayed up. I read it all.

I eagerly flipped through the pages at first. I heard about how Job was righteous and faithful, about how God boasted about his faithfulness. I read how Satan heard this and challenged God on it, saying that Job was only faithful because of all of the blessings God had given him in his life. At this pivotal point, God allows Satan to take away the blessings that God had given him. Satan believed that when Job was stripped of the comforts in his life, he would curse God instead. God allowed him to find out. That disturbed me, as it always does, giving God and Satan almost Greek god-like qualities in the way they fiddle with human frailties, but I read on. I read through the chapters as Job is stricken with illnesses, his home is destroyed, his farm is irreparably damaged, and his children are killed. He was devastated. He cried out to God. He was confused. His friends came to him and admonished him. They told him that he must be suffering right now because of his own sin. They said that God must be angry. For dozens of chapters, Job has long discussions with his well-meaning friends about the possible causes of his trials and ways they suggest he could rid himself of the sin that must have brought it all on. Job answers them with stories of his own righteousness and faith to God and disregards their thoughts. I then remember reading about the restoration of all that Job lost. I remember God relieving Job of his afflictions and again granting blessings. His life is restored.

At first that sounds nice. "Oh, thanks, God. You have restored what was lost." I read that, and then I got mad. Wow. First God plays with a righteous man, allows him to suffer to prove a point to Satan, allows his family to die before him and in the end says He will just restore it? That's absurd, I thought. I really had trouble sleeping then.

The next day was Monday, thankfully, and I got to talk it over with my Monday Night family, but we weren't Bible scholars then (and we aren't now either, by the way), so although I got to vent, I never did understand the lesson I could have been taking from Job. I was still angry. If Andy had to die, what kind of restoration would bring me joy again? Was this the comfort I could expect from the Bible? That's it? The idea was infuriating!

Since then I heard an incredible teaching on Job. The pastor recounted the story as one on humility, not one on trials. You see, in chapter 38 of Job, where God begins to answer the cries of Job on His own, it becomes obvious that God is teaching a lesson in humility. He is reminding Job, and not gently, that he was not there when He created the heavens and the earth. He reminds Job that he is just created, not Creator. Job is humbled. Only then is his life restored.

Still, I felt bothered by the idea that God would just restore lost loved ones to us and all would be as it was. Could God just replace Andy after he died? Would that ever be acceptable to me? Could I ever live with the idea that that's what God meant by restoration? No.

That's not how it all happened, though. It has been over three years now since Andy left this world.

I do still feel sadness; a gut-wrenching sorrow can still grip me, immobilize me. I still miss Andy, but I am able to work and enjoy my children and care for my home without being overwhelmed with grief. My joy has been restored.

My circumstances have changed: I am not battling breast cancer. My health has been restored.

My job is secure. I am able to manage my finances on my own. My financial stability has been restored.

My children are happy and healthy and growing up in the knowledge of the Lord. The worries that I held then are now gone. My prayers were answered. My faith is restored.

I can look to my future without fear or sorrow. My hope is restored.

Restoration may be more than God just giving us our comfort back. It is better than what I had before because of what I've learned. I value what God has given me. I understand what it's like not to have it.

And what about my husband? I feel like Dorothy at the last moments in "The Wizard of Oz" when she says, "Oh, there's nothing in that black bag for me." She feels that nothing could possibly be in the wizard's bag of tricks for her that would restore her to her home. You know the story. Dorothy does get home. She is correct that there's nothing the 'wizard' can do, but she is ultimately wrong. She has been given the power to get home all along.

I was wrong, too. No, God hasn't had Andy raised from the dead to achieve the kind of restoration in my life that I would've wanted. Even though Andy has not been miraculously brought back, God has restored my peace about that. I really do wish Andy were here with me still. I haven't stopped missing him. I just have traveled through those lost and lonely days of grieving with a God who stayed with me, comforted me; and now I know what God means by restoration. I have been given confidence in God's promises to stay beside me. Like Dorothy, I have also been given the power to live a restored life. Like ruby slippers on my very own feet, I have been given the ability to operate within the love of God. I have been taught that the love I had in my marriage to Andy is still here and is still a part of me, not on my feet exactly, but, you know what I mean.

EPILOGUE

It's the second of September, the last day of another summer writing. The book is finished. It will need editing and more organizing, but the bulk of the writing is done. School starts in a few days. School supplies are on the kitchen counter. The kids have their school clothes and new sneakers. It's time to change our shorts in for warm sweaters and to pile the wood by the back door for a fall and winter of warm, cozy fires in the living room. Seasons change.

I feel ambivalent. A finality has been washing over me. It makes me feel sad and relieved at once. I'm glad to feel a sense of completion, but I feel like I'm letting go of Andy now. I feel like I'm leaving these pages as his memory now, no more, no less, just what's in these pages. Maybe there's some truth in that. Maybe leaving the memories somewhere helps me to go on living.

Through this summer I've recalled the beautiful days of falling in love, the hard days of trial and forced perseverance and the confused days of loss and grief. I have allowed myself to sink back into each of those emotional moments so that I could share them here. It has been fruitful and painful at once. To recognize the magnitude of the loss hurts me all over again. I guess my memory had chosen to lose some of the details in an effort to carry on living, to believe that I am just fine without Andy. Writing it out has reminded me that I didn't used to feel able, that after Andy died the pain was so great that I couldn't imagine living without him or how to live in spite of the memories, so I wanted to just die, too.

Reflecting on it has helped me because now I can see how far I've come. I will always carry the sorrow from this loss. I will always be sad that Andy is not here, but I am able to smile more often, and I am able to live. Strangely, as I have been writing these last pages, I have been learning about love.

About six months after Andy died, I invited Andy's best friend Tony to come out one night and help Katie and I sort through some boxes of Andy's personal belongings. It was probably too soon to do something like that; it felt like we were rifling through his things. It was uncomfortable for all three of us, so much so that we wound up putting it all back in, snapping the lids on the air tight containers and stacking them in a big closet. It was on that night, though, that Tony repeated what he often repeated, "Listen, Catherine, you're only 38 years old. You're a healthy, beautiful young woman with your life ahead of you. You will find someone else. It may not happen right away, but trust me, Andy wouldn't want you to be alone and sad like this forever."

I looked over the pizza box and the glass of wine on the table and saw a man who loved Andy very much. He was doing what he felt Andy would have wanted him to do, what I imagine he would have wanted Andy to do for his own beloved wife, Denise, if the situation were reversed. He was trying to send me on my way back into living as he thought Andy wanted.

I repeated that night and in other similar conversations with Tony that Andy and I had discussed it. We had been driving alone in the car on the way to church one morning toward the end of his illness when he leaned in at a red light to give me a kiss. He grinned afterward and said, "No one else will ever kiss you like that" and he giggled. He thought it was funny, but they are lasting words. I questioned him about it then through our giggling, and his response was to sing a line from that Lou Rawls song, "You'll Never Find Another Love Like Mine"; and then he laughed some more.

I know that Andy was teasing me, but I also felt that he couldn't leave this world giving me a blessing to pursue love after he left. He was jealous. He had been young and vibrant, and it was him that I was in love with. He never did say that I should move on after he died. He didn't feel that way.

Tony understood the silliness of his friend, but also said that he knew Andy's heart. He held his ground and reiterated that Andy would not want me to spend my life alone out of grief. He knew that I would love again.

The truth is that I wanted to yell at Tony. I never would have because I understood the love for Andy that was spoken in his words. He really wanted me to know this truth and to live life again. I didn't want to. I wanted to yell because I didn't want to love again. I wanted Andy. I wasn't lonely; I missed Andy. I wasn't afraid of living without love; I was sad about living without Andy. The remedy could only be found in our reunion, not with me finding a different love. And besides, who could ever be to me what Andy had been? There's that Job again. How can God just promise to restore someone's life? How could he restore my life without resurrecting Andy?

But, as I shared before, God is a God of restoration. The scripture doesn't lie. This is a lesson I have learned slowly and painfully, but it is so. After three years, I can say that God is a God of restoration.

In fact, the process of writing this book has been a series of lessons. I have grown up in my faith, grown to love God and to remain faith-filled even in the face of unanswered prayer, even when I pray for my husband to be healed and he gets sicker, and still I plan a funeral.

I also learned to listen to God's voice. I have had enough successes and failures to feel confidence about knowing when to act on the prompting of the Holy Spirit.

I have learned how important the Word of God is. I have learned that if I truly want to know and understand God then I need to recognize His voice and set it apart. The best way to do this is to read the scripture that He's given us so that I know the words that God would use, so that I know God's heart and can recognize it in other places.

I learned that God doesn't have limits. Even though most of us are only comfortable with God being in church on Sunday and with us in our evening prayers, He isn't limited to being present just there. God can touch us in ways that don't include sermons and memorized prayers and rituals. God can be in our dreams, in our moment-to-moment communication with him throughout bad days -- and good ones. God can appear before us if He chooses, can send angels with messages, can send confirmations in any way He chooses. He is God. Don't I want to worship a limitless, powerful and even creative God? Even though it may be tough to discuss with those who have not yet experienced Him in this way, would I really want God to be bound to rules that humans are bound by? Limited by time and sound and gravity and a body?

As I spent this summer studying the Old Testament scripture more than I ever have, I heard loudly and clearly how powerful our God is. I read about a God that could provide nourishment for His people by raining food down daily from the sky. He could appear to us in fire, in pillars of clouds, whose voice could be heard audibly to those He chose to speak to and those who believed they could hear Him. He could flood the earth or send mercy and give second, third, fourth chances as He saw fit.

As is natural, I've been trying to apply God's Word to my own life. I've been recognizing times when I have been provided for, when instead of fresh manna raining down on me, the mailbox was full of donations. I've been recognizing times when God has spoken to me and directed me through visions and dreams and Spirit-led prayer. I've recognized times in my life when

I didn't listen to that direction, and what twists my life took when I chose to forge my own stubborn path. I've also been able to accept the concept of restoration, and I've learned to allow love back in.

You may have wondered: why the feet on the front cover? It seems odd at first, but the Bible is full of references about feet and about walking. It does make sense: walking by faith, not by sight; walking on water; walking on the straight and narrow; Jesus washing the feet of his disciples; and the nail wounds in Jesus' feet. As we walk through the journey that is our lives, as we hope that we stay on that straight and narrow, we keep walking. Sometimes we walk backward, sometimes we walk blind, sometimes we walk away in defiance, and sometimes we walk toward God and toward love and light and hope. Our faithful feet carry us through our days, one at a time. We can neglect them or nurture them, but we must allow them to carry us. They carry us through storms, through beautiful beach days, through every kind of weather. Our feet never know what kind of day they will get, but they walk on. With the cover, I honor my feet! I remember the way that Andy caressed my feet and showed love for me through his affection for and admiration of this base part of my body. I honor the walking that they do, the carrying on that they have done on rainy days and sunny days, when they have been forced to stay under me and sustain me even if I didn't have the will to rise up.

I must tell here of the Lord's faithfulness. My feet have been rewarded. On the front cover, the feet beside mine are not Andy's, but those of a new love brought to me by the grace of God, the feet of a man named Tom who has agreed to journey with me through my grieving, believing that I can keep walking, and praying that we will walk together through the next chapters of our lives. Restoration.

CPSIA information can be obtained
at www.ICGtesting.com
Printed in the USA
BVOW03s2135210917
495579BV00001B/41/P